Pressing Toward the Marks of Ministerial Leadership

Theoretical Frameworks and Workshop Exercises

Lorrie C. Reed, M.Div., Ph.D.

Unless otherwise indicated, all scriptural references are from the Holy Bible, NKJV, NRSV, or NLT.

ISBN: 978-1-7372233-1-3

Publisher: Center Street Publishing, LLC
P.O. Box 438534
Chicago, IL 60643

Dedication

For gifted leaders and other shepherds who have been called
into Christian ministry:

"What's that you have in your hand?"

God gets all the glory!

Acknowledgements

I am indebted to friends, family, and colleagues who invested their time in reviewing the manuscript-in-progress and providing useful comments and critiques. Specifically, I would like to thank Reverend Chuck Maney, a pastor emeritus from the Illinois Conference of the United Church of Christ, Reverend Ozzie Smith, Jr., Pastor Emeritus of Covenant United Church of Christ, Reverend Melody L. Seaton, senior pastor at Grace United Church of Christ, Reverend Donna Freeman, associate pastor at Grace United Church of Christ, Dr. Mary Allen Carey, professor emeritus in psychological nursing at University of Oklahoma, and Mrs. Valarie Cooper, MBA, MSW, a lay person and former administrative assistant in her community church; Val reviewed the manuscript with a keen editorial eye. I am always grateful for the love and support of my daughter, Tamara Reed Tran. All of you went above and beyond the usual in carefully reviewing the manuscript and providing helpful comments on how to improve it. I would also like to thank my husband, Deacon James Reed, for his unfailing support during this project and throughout my ministry. A special thanks to the School for Ministry student cohorts, who inspired this project.

Epigraph

Beloved, I do not consider that I have made it my own; but this one thing I do: forgetting what lies behind and straining forward to what lies ahead, I press on toward the goal for the prize of the heavenly call of God in Christ Jesus. (Philippians 3:13-14, NRSV)

Table of Contents

Preface

THE PURPOSE OF THIS BOOK

Pressing Toward the Marks of Ministerial Leadership is intended to help you broaden and deepen your awareness of what it means to be an effective ministerial leader in the 21st century. Chapters in this book provide an overview of theoretical frameworks and practical principles that have stood the test of time and are descriptive of what occurs in most organizational settings. Thought-provoking workshop exercises at the end of each chapter address the needs of adult learners and foster critical thinking, effective communication, and creativity, along with the ability to sustain effective and ethical relationships in evolving congregational settings. Examples in this book grow out of the author's experiences since 1980 as a researcher, leader, administrator, teacher/professor, ordained minister, and change agent. Major topics include the nature of your call to ministry, methods for theological reflection, and elements of Christian worship. Further, the book examines theoretical frameworks for leadership, administration, communication, and teaching, along with other processes associated with serving at the helm of an organization. As a result of reading this book, you will become better at problem-solving, analysis, spiritual self-empowerment, promoting justice, and developing critical consciousness about the linkages among faith, leadership, and service in your organizational setting.

STRATEGY OF THE BOOK

Most of the theorists and researchers cited in this book conducted their studies in educational settings initially. During my career in administration, I embraced these research-based frameworks, which I had learned about and practiced between 1980 and 1995 in my positions as consultant, associate principal, curriculum director, and later as a junior high school principal.

These propositions served me well. Between 1995 and 2004, as a university professor, I had the privilege of teaching these same theories to master's degree candidates who were working to fulfill the requirements for certification in educational administration. It came as no surprise to me that, when I was called into ministry, I was able to translate my knowledge, skills, and abilities across the board as an associate pastor and later as the director of a school for ministry. Now, I welcome the opportunity to share these insights with you with the hope that you will benefit from them in some meaningful way.

Granted, this book does not include the most recent theoretical frameworks or those that are the most popular. Rather, the theories included herein represent longstanding constructs that have stood the test of time and are descriptive of what occurs in many organizational settings. Throughout the book, I have replaced the designations of principal, teacher, stakeholder, and school with corresponding terms that may require clarification when used in ministry.

A *ministerial leader* is anyone who is in charge of a program in a congregational or non-congregational organization. This may include pastors, evangelists, Christian educators, ministers of music, youth ministers, parish nurses, chaplains, counselors, program administrators, and chairs of ministries and committees. The term may also include faculty or administrators in seminaries and other educational institutions that prepare leaders for work in ministry.

I use the term *organization* throughout this book to refer to "an organized body of people with a particular purpose, especially a business, society, association, etc.," as noted in the Oxford Languages Dictionary.[1]

The term *member* refers to any participant, parishioner, congregant, or stakeholder in the religious organizational setting.

ORGANIZATION OF THE BOOK

The content of this book is presented in ten chapters. **Chapter 1** covers *answering one's call to ministry*. **Chapter 2** discusses *managing change* in the church environment. **Chapter 3** introduces *theological reflection* and other tools to help ministerial leaders ground their practice in personal theology. **Chapter 4** provides an overview of *worship* and its major components, including prayer, preaching, and the eucharist. **Chapter 5** discusses *the care of self and others*. **Chapter 6** introduces strategies for effective *teaching and learning*. The emphasis is on teaching about justice. **Chapter 7** details the principles and processes of *effective communication*, which are critical for effective organizational functioning. **Chapter 8** focuses on *leadership in organizations* and outlines the skills and dispositions of an effective leader in today's ministerial settings. **Chapter 9** describes the realm of *administration* and offers tools for successful organizational management. This includes adherence to a ministerial code of ethics. **Chapter 10** introduces *strategic planning* and outlines step-by-step guidance on how to formulate a strategic plan. Additionally, each chapter ends with workshop exercises to reinforce understanding and practice. The book also provides resources participants may use to further explore the information covered in the chapters.

This book provides basic principles that will appeal to a broad spectrum of readers – those who have been in ministry for a while as well as those who have recently discerned a calling. Others who may benefit from reading this book include both ordained and lay **clergy, seminarians, students** in religious studies programs, **Christian educators, ministers of music, youth ministers, parish nurses, chaplains, and ministry chairs in congregational or non-congregational settings**. It may also be informative for **administrators** and **collegiate faculty** in seminaries and religious studies programs, who may wish to share the content with their students.

PART I: THE CALL TO MINISTERIAL SERVICE

Chapter 1: What is Your Call Story?

CHAPTER PREVIEW

Readings and exercises in this chapter will help you:

- Recognize the evolution of your sense of call.
- Continue discernment in community.
- Develop a healthy sense of self as shaped by God, community, and life experiences.

WHAT IS YOUR CALL STORY?

Most ministerial leaders have a call story to tell. Mine begins like this: "One day, I was sitting there minding my own business when... ." If you're like me, you were called out of one situation into another with little prior notice and a feeling that you were not equipped yet for the tasks you were to perform. Responding to the call affects people in different ways. For me, I felt the urge to embark upon a quest in search of my purpose in life. I didn't know what *it* was, but I sensed that I would know *it* when I saw *it*. The journey was marked by many twists and turns.

During my journey, I engaged in formal and informal education, while always paying attention to the commonalities across disciplines. As I studied the latest "-ologies" and "- isms," I learned to see the big picture. In the process, I developed problem-solving and analytical skills that helped me sort things out, and I acquired the ability to recognize and respond to challenging situations. I developed a stark awareness of what makes an organization thrive and what makes it falter.

Having served in the field of administration many years before my calling, I already possessed knowledge about these things. The difference between pre-call and post-call was that during my period of discernment, I was challenged to apply my knowledge, skills, and dispositions in new ways.

Countee Cullen, an American poet, novelist, children's writer, and playwright during the Harlem Renaissance wrote: "Yet Do I Marvel" in 1925. The poem recounted the mysteries of God - why the little buried mole continues blind, why flesh that mirrors Him must someday die, why Sisyphus was doomed to struggle up a never-ending stair. The poem ends in this way: "Inscrutable His ways are, and immune to catechism by our petty cares. Yet do I marvel at this curious thing: To make a poet black, and bid him sing!"

Today, I will borrow the phrase from this celebrated poet: Yet do I marvel at this curious thing: that God would call a person like me – and you – into ministry with only the skills we have picked up along the way and expect us to do the work of the Kingdom of God. We are not unique. When God called Moses at the burning bush, Moses was reluctant to answer the call because he did not think his abilities were adequate.

> *Then Moses answered, "But suppose they do not believe me or listen to me, but say, 'The LORD did not appear to you.'" The LORD said to him, "What is that in your hand?" He said, "A staff."* (Exodus 4:1-2, NRSV)

What's that you have in your hand? Think of it this way: The experiences you acquired before ministry served as a training ground for what you would be doing later. For example, God called me into ministry around 2001. By that time, my journey to discover my purpose had already taken me through many jobs, degrees, and experiences. Finally, when I stopped resisting and surrendered to the call, I had honed the ability to see the world through many lenses. For me, these views included K-12 teaching and administration, university teaching, consulting, in addition to ministry.

When I look back on it all, I perceive that everything I have done from my first job until now has prepared me for what I was to accomplish as the director of a ministry school. Even the challenges of my secular jobs equipped me for that sacred work because along the way I had developed strength, courage, stamina, and empathy, among other qualities. I learned how to survive and share my insights and strategies with others who also sought to engage in ministerial leadership.

My career as an administrator and leader goes back to 1980. In the beginning, there was so much I didn't know, and I still don't have most of the answers. But the nature and quality of my questions have changed radically since I first began this journey. Now, many years out of the starting block, I can draw on a rich cache of knowledge, wisdom, and understanding and translate my skill set to the work of ministry. The lessons I have learned have universal applicability. I am called to pass them along to you as you embark upon this awesome journey. I pray that sharing with you what I have learned may help you along the way.

WORKSHOP EXERCISES

8:30 a.m. – 9:00 a.m.	Invocation/Welcome Introductions/Community Building Creating a Hospitable Environment
9:00 a.m. – 12:00 noon	**Workshop Session 1** **Activity 1 – Scripture Analysis** **Activity 2 – Scripture Analysis**
12:30 p.m. – 1:00 p.m.	Lunch
2:00 p.m. – 5:00 p.m.	**Workshop Session 2** **Activity 1 – Scripture Analysis** **Activity 2 - Reflecting on your call**
5:30 p.m. – 6:00 p.m.	Workshop Evaluation, Closing Worship, Benediction, Dismissal

Learning Activity: Read Acts 16:6-15 (Paul's encounter with Lydia in Macedonia). The following assignment will help you reflect on your call. Jot down your responses to the questions presented.

- Who is being called?
- What are they being called to do?
- What is their response to the call?
- What is the ambiguity in each call?
- Is there hesitancy in the response? If so, describe.
- How, if at all, was each call confirmed?

Learning Activity: Read Genesis 12 (Abraham's call to Canaan).. The following assignment will help you reflect on your call. Jot down your responses to the questions presented.

- Who is being called?
- What are they being called to do?
- What is their response to the call?

- What is the ambiguity in each call?
- Is there hesitancy in the response? If so, describe.
- How, if at all, was each call confirmed?

Learning Activity: Read Ruth 1:1-18 (The story of Naomi and Ruth). The following assignment will help you reflect on your call. Jot down your responses to the questions presented.
- Who is being called?
- What are they being called to do?
- What is their response to the call?
- What is the ambiguity in each call?
- Is there hesitancy in the response? If so, describe.
- How, if at all, was each call confirmed?

Learning Activity: Read Luke 1:26-38 (Gabriel's call to Mary). The following assignment will help you reflect on your call. Jot down your responses to the questions presented.
- Who is being called?
- What are they being called to do?
- What is their response to the call?
- What is the ambiguity in each call?
- Is there hesitancy in the response? If so, describe.
- How, if at all, was each call confirmed?

Reflect on your call. Now reflect on your call. What do you perceive you are being called to do? What are the short-term and long-term implications of answering the call? What hesitancy do you have about your call? What invigorates you? Draw a picture that represents your call experience. Be prepared to share an account of your call story with your groupmates.

SUGGESTED RESOURCES

"Discerning Your Call and Your Gifts For Ministry of Word and Sacrament." Available from:
https://www.pcusa.org/site_media/media/uploads/prep4min/pdfs/discerning-your-call.pdf

"Discovering Your Spiritual Type." Available from
http://centraltolife.org/wp-content/uploads/2019/Documents/BibleStudies/Discover-Your-Spiritual-Type.pdf

"What is a 'call' to ministry?" Available at:
https://www.ucc.org/what-we-do/justice-local-church-ministries/local-church/mesa-ministerial-excellence-support-and-authorization/ask-the-question_q-a/

Chapter 2: Managing Change

CHAPTER PREVIEW

Readings and exercises in this chapter will help you:

- Heighten awareness of the need for systemic change in ministerial settings.
- Analyze the nature of systemic change.
- Examine the nature of change in churches.

EVERYTHING MUST CHANGE

A major theme of this book is managing the changes that inevitably occur in all organizations. From the moment you are born, you begin to change. It's all about maintaining optimal relationships, as our relationships are in a state of perpetual motion. Every time you congregate with new person, you discover that you must adjust your behavior to accommodate the needs of others in your environment. If yours is a healthy organization, just about everything you do will be geared toward bringing about growth and improvement in your relationships. You will also discover that inflexibility leads to conflict on many levels.

Think about the situations you find yourself in regularly in your ministerial setting. As a Sunday school teacher, you are in a position to influence students' understanding and to help them reflect on their perspectives and behavior. As the chairperson of the women's ministry, you may have to work to facilitate communication and agreement among the members on goals, objectives, and program outcomes. As an administrative assistant, you may need to document an evolving initiative, perhaps conferring with others along the way. All of these tasks involve change on some level.

As the leader of a congregation, you will need to keep the organizational vision in the forefront, constantly inspiring and motivating others to move the organization closer to where it is called to be. The organizational mission and vision must form the foundation of your change process. A carefully articulated mission and vision will provide a clear look at the big picture (more about this in Chapter 10). Sometimes leaders and organizations have poorly focused targets at which to aim. Without such visual and conceptual goals, the organization is likely to experience ceaseless fluctuation that keeps you from moving forward. Until the focus becomes clear, trying to improve relationships and operations in ministerial settings will remain little more than the practice of shooting arrows into the wind and hoping they land somewhere near the intended mark. Your change efforts must be systemic.

For purposes of this discussion, *systemic change* is defined as holistic self-examination, redefinition, renewal, or reformulation of fundamental principles, beliefs, and practices that drive the entire organization toward the attainment of its goals. Such an encompassing definition is based in part on the notion that most organizations exist in an *open system,* with a dynamic interchange between internal and external environmental influences. To maintain equilibrium in such an environment, ministerial organizations have to adapt practices that contribute to their survival - a notion that is referred to as *organizational resiliency* in the present discussion.

Organizational resiliency takes into account the synergistic impact of any organizational adjustment, which is here referred to as *organizational ecology.* Ministerial settings that are kept off-balance cannot concentrate for sustained periods on goal attainment. Therefore, the organization needs to engage in practices geared toward organizational self-renewal; this, in turn, which results in a movement toward goal attainment and in the survival of the organism.

Viewing a phenomenon from a systems perspective draws our attention to the influence of the larger environment, the complex interdependencies that exist within that environment, and the impact of subtle changes on the organism as a whole. In the light of systems theory, cause-effect relationships become problematic – a single factor is rarely the cause of an outcome; rather, the cause is associated with an intricate and sensitive interplay of subsystems within the larger entity. Thus, the concept of subsystems is coupled with that of multiple-causation, and together they become central to systems thinking.[2]

In ministerial settings, this balancing act is associated with an endless, cyclical transaction between the setting and the surrounding environment, a transaction in which organizational behavior is contingent upon forces that extend beyond the self-contained context of the setting. In this view, you must understand that change in any setting requires you to examine the relationships between human behavior and the context (environment, ecology) that are characteristic of the organization.[3] Feedback can come from many sources including action research, attitude inventories, case studies, focus groups, interviews, observations, portfolios, program evaluation, public forums, questionnaires, surveys, and the leading of the Holy Spirit.

Resistance to Change

As articulated earlier in this chapter, change is inevitable. However, the average person is resistant to change. If you are like most people, you have some fear of the unknown. You prefer to operate within the status quo because it is safe. Other people may perceive change as a threat to their power or influence. Typically, change requires you to do something different and could end up making your knowledge and skills obsolete. In the minds of many people, it is easier to stay where you are.

Kurt Lewin's Force-field Analysis

A social scientist by the name of Kurt Lewin described a method for managing change. He called it Force Field Analysis.[4] Although his model was developed in 1951, it still holds relevance for today's ministerial leaders. According to Lewin, most entities exist in a state of quasi-equilibrium; that is, a temporary balance of factors until the next change occurs. He said that initiating change requires movement – from one state to another. To get to the new state, you need to unfreeze the current situation, move it in deliberate ways, and refreeze it when the desired change has occurred.

The chart on the next page describes this process. As shown in the chart, during the *unfreezing* stage, ministerial leaders must demonstrate how conditions or data support the change. The change, for example, may require altering values, attitudes, or beliefs. The *moving* stage requires developing new values, implementing new programs, restructuring jobs or lives, and implementing a comprehensive plan. As you engage in ushering in the new, you must strengthen the forces that drive change and weaken the forces that stand in the way. Finally, in the *refreezing stage*, you will engage in activities aimed at stabilizing the change at a new quasi-stationary equilibrium. You will do this by implementing a supportive culture, nurturing structures, and providing opportunities for people to build their capacity to sustain the desired innovation.

Change in Churches

The need for change in church organizations is ongoing, inevitable, and driven by social, political, and economic factors at any given time. From my perspective as a researcher and minister, I have noticed that change tends to affect every aspect of the religious environment and has the potential to throw off-balance the delicate ecology of the organization. Until congregations and other faith-based entities have a way of monitoring the ecological impact of change on outcomes, they will continue to operate with uncertainty, leaving largely up to chance what many people see as the one best hope for people in despair.

At the same time, leaders in ministerial settings are compelled to walk by faith and not by sight. They must leave room for the movement of the Holy Spirit. The church is called to be many things to many people, but, taking my cues from the medical profession, I believe that we in the body of Christ must "first, do no harm." As an effective ministerial leader, you must develop a critical awareness of the impact of what you do on the outcomes you desire. The frameworks presented in this book can serve as navigational tools to help you steer away from danger.

Kurt Lewin's Force Field Analysis (1951)

Unfreezing
Demonstrating how conditions and data support change such as altering values, attitudes, beliefs
Moving
Developing new values, implementing new programs, restructuring roles, implementing a comprehensive plan
Strengthening the driving forces
Weakening the restraining forces
Refreezing
Stabilizing change at a new quasi-stationary equilibrium, nurturing structure, culture, and capacity

Assumptions about Change

Change theorist Michael Fullan has studied change extensively[5] and has identified ten assumptions about change that the ministerial leaders should consider.

1. Do not assume that your version of what the change should be is the one that should be implemented.
2. Do not assume that the reason for lack of implementation is outright rejection of the values embodied in the change or hard-core resistance to all change. There are a number of possible reasons: value rejection, inadequate resources to support implementation, insufficient time elapsed.
3. Do not expect all or even most people or groups to change. Progress occurs when you take steps that increase the number of people who support the new ideas.
4. Assume that any significant innovation, if it is to result in change, requires individual implementers to work out their own meaning.
5. Assume that conflict and disagreement are not only inevitable, but fundamental to successful change.
6. Assume that people need pressure to change (even in directions that they desire). But it will only be effective under conditions that allow them to react, to form their own position, to interact with other implementers, to obtain technical assistance, etc.
7. Assume that effective change takes time: 3 - 5 years for specific innovations, greater than 5 years for institutional reform.
8. Assume that changing the culture of institutions is the real agenda, not implementing single innovations.
9. Assume that no amount of knowledge will ever make it totally clear what action should be taken.
10. Assume that you will need a plan that is based on the above assumptions.

Why the Church Needs to Change

In an environment where everything has to be fabulously grotesque, extravagantly diverse, intensely scary, or extremely marginal, what should the 21st-century church look like? How should we *do* church in the present day? How do we structure our programs and services in an environment that is in a constant state of transition? According to recent research, the church requires radical change and healing from the outside as well as from the inside out. The approach of this book is to help motivate justice-minded people to dig a little deeper and look a little closer at the issues of concern. Identify the factors that have an impact on change, and prayerfully address them. The task might require stirring up a little cognitive dissonance and making inconsistencies plain so that a runner can read them! (Habakkuk 2:2). Change is ongoing, and so must be our efforts to manage it.

WORKSHOP EXERCISES

8:30 a.m. – 9:00 a.m.	Invocation/Welcome Introductions/Community Building Creating a Hospitable Environment
9:00 a.m. – 12:00 noon	**Workshop Session 1** **Activity 1 – Force Field Analysis** **Activity 2 – Resisting Change**
12:30 p.m. – 1:00 p.m.	Lunch
2:00 p.m. – 5:00 p.m.	**Workshop Session 2** **Activity 1 – Open Systems** **Activity 2 – Case Study Analysis**
5:30 p.m. – 6:00 p.m.	Workshop Evaluation Closing Worship, Benediction, Dismissal

Learning Activity: Using Kurt Lewin's force-field analysis model, diagnose your organization. Think about a change that needs to be made in your setting. Identify the driving forces for change and the forces that resist change. What will it take to implement positive change in your organization?

Learning Activity: Why do people in your particular setting resist change? Describe a situation in which people in your setting resisted change. What strategies did the ministerial leaders use to overcome resistance to change? What more, if anything could have been done?

Learning Activity: What does an open system look like in your ministerial setting? Describe the components of the open system. Are they religious, secular, or other. What are some of the other variables that religious institutions have to take into account?

Learning Activity: Now think about your unique setting. Briefly describe a personal experience you had in managing or facilitating change. What was rewarding about your experience? What was challenging?

Case Study: The New Pastor
Calvary Church had been founded in the early 1930s, primarily to serve the needs of five families, who valued a closed community and embraced traditional ways of worship. Over time, the priorities and interests of the congregation began to change as regentrification drove new members to settle in the community. When the church's long-standing pastor passed away suddenly, a search committee began looking for a replacement. The search and call process had been long and contentious. The committee failed repeatedly to agree on the characteristics they desired in a new pastor. Disagreements and tensions between the old guard and the newcomers threatened to tear the church apart. While older members on the committee wanted to hold onto their former practices, newer members valued contemporary ways of being the church.

In the past 10 years, the church had gone through three pastors before they finally called the Rev. Monica Chapman to lead the congregation. On her first day on the job, Rev. Monica walked to the door with two boxes balanced, one on top of the other. Concentrating hard on not dropping them, she fumbled in her purse to retrieve the building keys the conference administrator had left in her possession. She didn't have to fumble too long, for Charlie, the custodian, met her at the front door.

"Let me help you with that," he said as he relieved her of one of the boxes.

"Thanks. Good morning," she replied.

Charlie escorted Rev. Monica to her office. "I was working on the floors in the fellowship hall when I saw you drive up," Charlie explained. "I still have the kitchen to strip and wax before I'm done down there. I'm working by myself today, but if you need anything, just holler."

"Thanks, I'll do that," she replied as she placed her boxes on the desk.

Rev. Monica walked around the building noting many things that she would like to change, giving no thought to why certain things were situated as they were. Pride swelled inside her. This church was now her building, and she intended to make her mark on the parishioners and the surrounding community. She was there to make a difference – become part of the legend, so to speak.

Back in her own office now, she heard a knock on the door.

"Hello." A voice called from the doorway.

"Hello. Come in." Rev. Monica responded.

"Welcome. I'm Rebecca Anderson, and I'm in charge of the Women's Auxiliary."

"It is so good to meet you." Rev. Monica held out her hand, which Rebecca grasped enthusiastically.

"I thought I'd stop by and help you get oriented for the church meeting on Friday night. You won't have to worry about our auxiliary; we've got it all under control," Rebecca said. "But there are some other ministries in this church that need a lot of

help. I guess that's where you come in. I hope you have better
luck than your predecessors. In any event, I brought you some
coffee. I hope you like it black and strong. That's how I take
mine."

***

On Friday night, Rev. Monica flashed her most welcoming
smile as she stood at the entrance to fellowship hall greeting
people waiting to enter the space. All the while, Rev. Monica
had her eye trained on a woman who for the past ten minutes
had propped her slight body against a bookcase down the hall
in the narthex. The woman glared at every passerby. With eyes
squeezed into almond-shaped slits and lips pursed tautly, she
sized things up, reconnoitered; then she prepared for the kill.
She moved forward deliberately, slowly at first, winding her way
through the crowd with her sights trained on the target. She
came to a halt directly in front of Rev. Monica.

"Hello. I'm Rev. Monica Chapman, the new pastor here."

"I know who you are," the woman snarled in a husky tone
through gritted teeth. The woman simply stared at Rev.
Monica's extended arm and open hand, to no avail. After a
couple of seconds, Rev. Monica allowed her arm to drop
without the satisfaction of being grasped in welcome.

"My name is Betty Williams, and my family and I have been
members of this church for 30 years."

"I'm looking forward to meeting your family."

"You probably are," Betty said. Then she paused and
looked around before she whispered. "No one wanted you here,
you know. You're the fourth pastor this church has had in 10
years. You need to watch your step because I'll be watching
you."

"My door is always open," Rev. Monica responded.
"Would it be possible for you to stop by the office on Monday
after 9 o'clock? I'd be happy to talk with you about your
concerns." Rev. Monica observed that the line behind Betty was

getting longer, so she brought the conversation to a close. "It was so nice to meet you, Mrs. Williams."

Once again, Rev. Monica held out her hand. Betty stared at it as if it were infected. Then she walked away, bumping into other parishioners who were waiting in line to meet the new pastor.

Rev. Monica signaled to Rebecca, who was standing on the other side of the room. As Rebecca made her way to where the new pastor was standing, Rev. Monica took a deep breath.

"Can you take over for a minute? I think I need a break," Rev. Monica mumbled to Rebecca. Rev. Monica stumbled toward her office for a short reprieve. She could see that stepping into the new position was not going to be easy.

Case Study Analysis Guidelines

1. What are the presenting problems as they relate to the topic of change? Define the nature of the problem(s).
2. Using relevant details from the case, identify the deeper issues if any. Evaluate the seriousness of the issues.
3. Determine the extent to which some kind of action is required immediately.
4. Identify two or more alternative solutions based on your analysis and theological reflection.
5. Describe a plan to implement your solution.

SUGGESTED RESOURCES

"It's a Whole New World." Available at:
https://www.ucc.org/vitality_ready-set-grow_know-community-culture_its-a-whole-new-world/

"6 Tips for Managing Change in the Church." Available at
https://smartchurchmanagement.com/6-tips-for-managing-change-in-the-church/

"Leading Change in the Church." Available at
https://anthonyhilder.com/leading-change-in-the-church/

Chapter 3: Reflecting Theologically

CHAPTER PREVIEW

Readings and exercises in this chapter will help you:
- Describe the use of theological reflection.
- Reflect theologically on your experiences.
- Practice a range of ways for engaging in reflection.

REFLECTING THEOLOGICALLY

Theological reflection is a useful tool to help you clarify your purpose, make decisions, and enact solutions based on God's plan for you and your ministry. Praying and seeking clarity through theological reflection will facilitate your movement "from the presenting problem to seeing the deeper issue and ultimately into dealing with the theological issue behind the deeper issue."[6]

Theological Reflection Models

Many models exist as frameworks for theological reflection. For this chapter, I have chosen models from Andrews University and Fuller Seminary. The models have similarities and differences. After reading about them, you should identify one (or combination) that is comfortable for you.

Andrews University

The Andrews University Doctor of Ministry program provides an example of how to do a theological reflection.[7] According to their definition, theological reflection "acknowledges God's movement in all of life, thus these sources are each respected. Theological reflection becomes an ongoing contribution, and critical thinking an ongoing part of the minister's reflective life."[8] The Andrews University writers assert that without a theological reflection model, people engaged in ministry tend to make decisions disconnected from "divine revelation and spiritually grounded experience." Hence, the writers define theology as the process of faith-seeking understanding.[9] Accordingly:

> *When a believer accepts the Bible as authoritative, theology is centered in the process of reflecting on and applying biblical truth to a particular situation. This interactive reflective process involves scripture, beliefs of the church, the one who seeks understanding, culture, and the specific ministry context to which theological reflection is applied.*[10]

In their view, the process of doing theology involves five key elements; namely, (a) biblical knowledge and understanding, (b) self-knowledge and awareness, (c) knowledge of the history and culture of the issue's context, (d) seeking to understand how God is at work in the present situation, and (e) reflecting critically with guidance by God's presence. According to the authors, "in-depth understandings of these five elements combine to form the raw material of theology. The more perceptive and careful we are on each element the more insightful and helpful is our theology."[11] The whole process entails engaging in personal, spiritual, and theological contemplation that involves examining the literature and other sources.

Fuller Seminary

Scott Cormode[12] from Fuller Seminary presented an overview of his theological reflection process. He says there are two goals of doing such reflection: (a) to make spiritual sense of a situation and (b) to determine how to respond to a situation. He asserted that engaging in reflection of this nature helps you clarify a given situation and respond appropriately. For ministerial leaders, the response arising from your theological consideration will represent your spiritual understanding of the problem and facilitate your ability to communicate an action to address the concern in question.

Cormode suggests that you prepare yourself with attitudes for reflection before engaging in the work. He offers three conditions of preparation. First, as with most other communication, you begin by listening. This means paying attention to the context of the problem or issue by looking at the cultural environment that shaped the situation and people involved. Next, you should listen to the community or the congregation from which the concern arises. You should listen to scripture and the Holy Spirit through acts of prayer. In this regard, listening becomes a spiritual activity because you are listening for God in addition to listening to other voices. Listening to God will require ongoing spiritual formation by cultivating individual disciplines as well as disciplines such as worship, journaling, sabbath, and others. Finally, you must learn "self-skills" in preparing for theological reflection. Self-skills include the following:[13] Self-reflection: being able to look back on the *past* and learn from what you did well and what you did poorly. Self-awareness: being able to understand how in this present moment you are being received by those around you and how your emotions and experiences are affecting your actions. Self-discipline: being able to follow through on a decision to act differently in the future.

Additional Reflective Tools

Not only can reflection be used in formal theological settings, but it can also help people to resolve unfinished business. After reflection, those issues that may have weighed you down so heavily before will be reduced to something manageable as you examine them in a different light. Both you and the issues will have a new identity and a new direction, in other words.

Additionally, reflecting represents an act of creativity. It is during this creative process that you have an opportunity to express heightened awareness of your situation and your relationship with God and other people. The more clarity you gain, the more empowered you feel. In the process, your sacred identity increases along with your spiritual self-concept. Several processes are available for people who wish to use these tools for personal growth. Some of them include poetry, storytelling, dance, music, art, sports, physical exercise, recreation, and prayer. I describe some of these tools below. Feel free to use the method of release that works best for you.

Using Journaling as a Reflective Tool

Journaling can serve as a mechanism through which people can interrogate their feelings and beliefs in an attempt to make sense of their lives. Journaling entails soul-wrenching introspection, helping the writer not only ask but also answer questions. Both liberating and empowering, journaling can work as a catalyst for personal growth and actualization. It represents a means for restoring memory, and the whole exercise can be therapeutic. Journaling allows you to put your thoughts and feelings on paper and to examine them later. It allows you to explore your innermost feelings in a private and safe place. You can ramble, doodle, and ignore the conventions of proper grammar if you wish. The thing to remember is that this process gives you a forum to purge, cleanse, and get it all out of your system and not have to be concerned with judgment from others.

Using Storytelling as a Reflective Tool

Storytelling is a time-honored tradition in many cultures. Stories convey important information in ways that few other forms of communication can accomplish. During storytelling, a shift in consciousness takes place, for your remembrances take on a narrative structure that might otherwise seem random and meaningless. With each re-telling, you can add new details to the old memories and deepen the context of what occurred and why. As you reconstruct and reconcile the information, you are forced to get the story straight as you fill in the gaps. In that regard, storytelling helps the mind to make sense of the world. Stories help both tellers and listeners to reconsider lived experiences in light of new possibilities. In addition, stories represent mechanisms for transmitting knowledge, wisdom, and hope from one generation to the next.

Using Poetry as a Reflective Tool

Unlike the typical prose form, which is fine for business reports and news stories, the everyday language you use is subjective, ambiguous, and embedded in highly personal contexts. In the discourse about personal matters, some of the images and experiences you wish to communicate may be too painful, too shameful, or too personal to convey with mere prose. Experiences that gave rise to these images live in vivid color and granulated texture in the places where your memories are stored. More often than not, simple prose is powerless to relate the spiritual essence of the messages you wish to express. Consequently, when dealing with abstract concepts, lofty ideals, or charged emotions, a prose form may be viewed as a factor that complicates mutual understanding.

Poetic communication, on the other hand, is the language that breaks things down to their essential meanings—stripped of their judgments and cultural baggage. If the message of the poem is true, its essence will serve as the skeletal structure on which the readers will add flesh, and dress, and color, and texture from their frames of reference. In this society that values rational, objective expression, you may not be able to write an essay about our concerns; nor are you certain that you understand the facets enough to organize them into a coherent piece of prose. But deep down inside you know how you feel, you know where you hurt, you understand the incongruence of the situation. Expressing all this succinctly through prose is sometimes impossible. Poetry gives you space to express that which would otherwise be ineffable.

Using Prayer as a Reflective Tool

When people talk to each other, they have a better sense of who they are concerning the other. If this talk does not occur, misunderstanding often results and signals get crossed. The same is true of your communication with God. The more you talk to God, the more acute is your understanding of God. The better you understand God, the more you are likely to trust. And if you can trust, you learn to wait and be still for God's response. From a practical standpoint, prayer allows you to let go of your anger, frustration, bitterness, resentment, or whatever negative energy you are harboring. As you release that energy in prayer, God restores you to equilibrium and gives you renewed reasons to hope.

Metacognition

As future ministerial leaders, you must keep in touch with your thinking about your practice and how that relates to the broader context. Thinking about your own thinking is called *metacognition*. Keeping a metacognitive journal will help you sort through the various issues you are likely to encounter as you begin to manage other people and situations. It is almost intuitive that thinking about your thinking through journaling always facilitates your personal and professional growth.

Not only that; when you sit in the head office, others will be concerned about what you think. People you manage will view your perspectives critically. Because so many people are watching you, you should sort out ahead of time what you believe and be able to state it clearly and succinctly whenever you are called on to do so.

Metacognitive analysis may require you to keep a daily electronic journal in which you record your thoughts, reactions, problems, issues, concerns, and other ideas that emerge. Your journal will probably include sketches, concepts, schedules, production materials, notes, observations, reflections, and ideas about your progress in dealing with your issue. Thinking about your thinking will place you ahead of the game.

WORKSHOP EXERCISES

8:30 a.m. – 9:00 a.m.	Invocation/Welcome Introductions/Community Building Creating a Hospitable Environment
9:00 a.m. – 12:00 noon	**Workshop Session 1** **Activity 1 – Case Study** **Activity 2 – Andrews Model**
12:30 p.m. – 1:00 p.m.	Lunch
2:00 p.m. – 5:00 p.m.	**Workshop Session 2** **Activity 1 – Case Study** **Activity 2 – Other Reflective Tools**
5:30 p.m. – 6:00 p.m.	Workshop Evaluation Closing Worship, Benediction, Dismissal

Learning Activity: Reflection Exercise – "The Repast"
The family had decided to hold Big Mama's repast on Walter Lee and Mabel's property. The weeds had been newly mowed for the gathering. Family members and friends sat around folding tables, laughing and telling stories to celebrate the life of the family's matriarch. In Mississippi fashion, they had prepared

a feast of fried chicken, collard greens, cornbread, macaroni and cheese, two kinds of punch and peach cobbler for dessert. There was a place at the community table for everyone, including the meat man and the milk man. The mail man and the insurance man enjoyed equal status, as did the neighborhood vagabond, Mr. Nelson, who pulled his little red wagon up and down the street, as he begged for anything he could recycle.

Over the years, Big Mama had been a kind of keeper of the collective memory. She was one of those people who knew things that stretched back for an eternity. She had head knowledge, but also, she possessed a deep-down wisdom that stretched way back, as if her spirit were connected with all the spirits who had ever lived. She had told the stories to the others, and they repeated them now, as they studied the old daguerreotype pictures family members had packed away in their satchels and shoe boxes as they traveled to their new home. Hannah didn't know who the people in the photographs, but she was struck by their stiff demeanors and the sadness in their eyes. They wore their Sunday's best and stood proudly, almost defiantly, to show that their existence mattered.

They told about the time Cousin Josephine died. They said her heart just stopped. You know hearts were never meant to tick forever. Now that Josephine was something else! A few years before they all left Mississippi, she lost all four of her grandsons to a lynch mob. They strung them up on tree limbs outside the courthouse. The ring leaders shot all of them – one at a time over a three-hour period, even though the boys had been dead since noon. They burned their bodies and dismembered them, passing out their severed limbs as souvenirs to the cheering crowd.

Hannah listened in amazement as they recalled the time Josephine had a nervous breakdown after the death of her boys and how her faith had sustained her. She'd given birth to twelve children altogether, and in doing so, her downline had avoided extinction. Her children were alive as long as their memories lived on, as they did at the repast. Oh, the stories they told... the social analysis that took place when a saint went home to be with God. The only exit from this life was through death, no matter what your background. If you were lucky, you story was added to the canon, like a collection of dots that connected humanity from everlasting to everlasting. They told stories about Big Mama. Every once in a while, she went missing. At first her absence frightened everyone. It didn't take long for us to realize, however, when Big Mama found life to be bothersome, she simply put on her hat, tied up a few things in a bundle, and start walking South, headed back home to Clarksdale, where the devils were known and the troubles predictable. Today she was going home for good.

That afternoon, they also talked about the lynching of a young boy in Money, Mississippi, the year before. Hannah was four years old with Emmett till was murdered in August 1955. They had all seen accounts of the massacre in *Ebony* and *Jet* Magazine. Reports of it were broadcast on the radio. Today, Hannah noticed that people seemed to be overwhelmed with sadness as they recounted the details of the gruesome encounter. She heard an undeniable intensity in the whispers and saw a terseness in their postures as they talked about the incident. And then they fell into silence.

After the church folks left, Uncle Taylor, pulled out the Bourbon whiskey. And somebody put on some blues music. There was laughing and drinking and dancing. After all, the occasion was a home-going – no sad tears to be found. The talking got louder, the laughing became more raucous, and the light-hearted signifying began, fueled on by the whiskey and the need to shake off their grief.

Walter Lee and Uncle Taylor had an ongoing rivalry. Every chance they got, they tried to outdo each other, vying for the designation of the "biggest and baddest." Their contest had been going on since they were young boys. They competed at gin rummy. They competed at betting on horse racing. They competed in horseshoes and checkers. Today, they were in a competition over trivia from the past.

"Speaking of Emmet Till," Walter said, "Didn't Cousin Ida used to life in Money, Mississippi?"

"No," Uncle Taylor replied. "She was from Itta Bena, Mississippi, over there close to Memphis."

"No, Walter replied. "I'm pretty sure it was Money."

"You old fool! You don't know what you're talking about."

"Well, look who's talking! You're too drunk to know the difference." Walter replied.

That's when they got up in each other's faces and started cussing. They could cuss! Before long they were throwing blows at each other, none of which landed where they was intended. Both brothers were breathing hard by then. Soon afterwards their energy was spent, as they toppled to the ground in a hangover-induced state of unconsciousness.

Case Analysis: Andrews Model for Theological Reflection
Using the model from Andrews University, reflect theologically on the case above (or a case of your own). Keep in mind the process they suggest. Consider the following:
1. Biblical knowledge and understanding
2. Self-knowledge and awareness
3. Knowledge of the history and culture of the issue's context
4. Understanding of how God is at work in the situation
5. Reflecting critically with guidance by God's presence

Case Study: Presiding Over Death
Each day from morning to afternoon, Chaplain Carrie Mae kept vigil, presiding over Andrew's death. There was something sacred about keeping watch over the transition of one of God's beloved. Through it all, she kept trying to get the story straight in her head. So, she wrote things down. She watched and prayed. And intermittently, she read scripture aloud. Usually from the

Psalms. Sometimes she read from one of the Gospels. She read to Andrew because she had heard somewhere that, for members in Andrew's state, the hearing was the last to go. Sometimes her lips barely moved. But she knew he could hear her. Faith comes by hearing.

After forty days, Andrew made his transition.

"The Lord gives. The Lord takes. Blessed by the name of the Lord." She whispered to herself.

That afternoon, Carrie Mae returned home from the hospital and had a meltdown. So many times, in the past year she had felt frustration and sometimes stress as she tried to understand why a man so young and vibrant should have to die in the crossfire of gun violence. On some days, Carrie Mae didn't know where she got the strength to keep giving to others. She often thought of herself as inadequate as she listened to their troubles. She had given others all she had. She had nothing else to offer. *How am I to get through all of this?* She asked herself daily.

Although tears welled up in Carrie Mae's eyes, she commanded them to recede and join their companions that had accumulated in her endless sea of weariness. There they waited – in the back of her mind, the bottom of her heart, and the pit of her soul – for permission to overflow.

Case Study Analysis Guidelines
Using one of the reflection tools you learned about in this chapter, reflect critically on the case above. How can you make spiritual sense of the situation? Do you agree with the way Carrie Mae handled the situation? If not, how would you have done it differently? How is God at work in this situation?

SUGGESTED RESOURCES

"Resources for Theological Reflection and Spiritual Support." Available at: https://divinity.yale.edu/news-media/news/yds-crisis-response/covid-19-updates-resources/resources-theological-reflection-and-spiritual-support

"A Framework for Theological Reflection." (Methodist Theological School) Available at: https://www.mtso.edu/site/assets/files/1136/framework_for_theological_reflection.pdf

"Models of Theological Reflection." (Loyola Marymount University). Available at: https://digitalcommons.lmu.edu/cgi/viewcontent.cgi?article=1032&context=ce

PART II: SHEPHERDING THE PEOPLE

Chapter 4: Preparing for Worship

CHAPTER PREVIEW

Readings and exercises in this chapter will help you:

- Describe the purpose and elements of worship.
- Affirm diverse practices in worship.
- Prepare a sermon for use in worship.
- Describe the importance of baptism, the Eucharist, and prayer in the context of worship.

THE BASIC COMPONENTS OF WORSHIP

According to Merriam-Webster, *worship* is defined as (1) reverence offered a divine being or supernatural power; an act of expressing such reverence. (2) a form of religious practice with its creed and ritual. (3) extravagant respect or admiration for or devotion to an object of esteem worship of the dollar.[14] The *Book of Worship* from the United Church of Christ notes,

> *"Christian worship is more than a passive response to God's revelation. It is in itself a Pentecostal proclamation. It both announces the good news of God's love for all the world and invites all people to share God's saving embrace."*[15]

Christian worship involves praising God in music and speech, readings from scripture, prayers of various sorts, sermons, and sacraments such as the Eucharist and Baptism. This chapter will describe elements of worship or liturgy.

Typical Components of Worship or Liturgy

Worship and liturgy are used synonymously in this chapter. *Westminster Dictionary of Theological Terms* defines the word *liturgy* as "work of the people." It is the sacred service of God offered by the people of God in divine worship.[16] The liturgy as worship service includes praise, adoration, thanksgiving, and petition directed toward God through actions and attitudes.

Worship practices vary widely depending on one's denomination, the setting, the culture, and many other long-held traditions. The United Church of Christ suggests that some of the following components might be included in a brief service of word and sacrament. If you are interested in reading a detailed explanation of each of these components, you can find them in the *Book of Worship* for the UCC.[17]

Greeting
Sentences of Adoration
Invitation
Confession of Sin
Assurance of Pardon
Hymn on Adoration
Reading Scripture
Sermon
Affirmation of Faith
Prayers of the People
Offertory
Passing of the Peace
Communion Prayer
Breaking Bread and Pouring Wine
Prayer of Our Savior
Sharing the Elements
Prayer of Thanksgiving
Commissioning
Benediction

Looking at it another way, worship comprises entering God's presence, listening to God, and responding to God. Entering God's presence may include a call to worship or invocation, a statement of call and response. This phase of worship might include a hymn of praise or other music. Approaching God and entering God's presence may also involve confession of sin, prayer, and assurance of pardon. Thanksgiving, praise offering, congregational concerns and pastoral prayer (intercessory prayer) may also be included. Listening to God entails scripture reading along with a sermon. Responding to God and one another includes fellowship and commitment to go forth to serve. In many settings, all of this is followed by an invitation, blessing, and benediction.

Observance of the Sacraments

Observing the Sacraments comprise an important part of the worship experience. Since the times of the ancient church, baptism has served as a rite of initiation into the community of faith. After baptism, Christians are permitted to receive the Eucharist, which puts them in communion with the church and other members of the body of Christ. Most denominations recognize Baptism and the Eucharist as Sacraments, which are celebrated in the presence of the community in the context of the worship service. Jesus mandated both Baptism and the Eucharist, and these sacraments "have been performed in expectation of certain promised benefits, specifically the forgiveness of sins, new life, and salvation."[18]

Baptism

Baptism means many things to various people. Since the times of the ancient church, baptism has served as a rite of initiation into the community of faith. In general, the word *baptism* means the rite of washing with water as a sign of religious purification and consecration. In the New Testament, baptism was equated

with repentance and forgiveness of sins (Mark 1:4). John the
Baptist, for example, performed the rite as a way of getting
people to acknowledge their sins, this was done in preparation
to receive forgiveness through the profession of faith and the
coming of the Messiah. In another sense, baptism represents a
way for Christians to participate in the death and resurrection
of Jesus Christ (Rom 6:1-11). In the contemporary view, one
becomes a member of the church by being baptized. In this
regard, baptism represents the boundary between being an
"outsider" and being an 'insider" in the Christian community. [19]

Eucharist

The word *Eucharist* carries many names and meanings. The word
Eucharist itself is from the Greek "thanksgiving." *Koinonia,* from
the Greek, is another word that denotes communion, which
implies sharing or participation, while the term *the Lord's Supper*
brings to mind a lavish feast. Eucharist entails the act of eating
and drinking together to commemorate the death and
resurrection of Christ. For some people, the Eucharist also
symbolizes charity and the eradication of injustice, poverty,
racism, brokenness, and metaphorical bondage, which plague an
entire underclass of people in America. When we engage in
"authentic communion," we are sharing our bounty (in the form
of a common meal), by bringing into the community the voices
of the poor and the weak with full conviction and attention to
their needs. Moreover, communion provides an opportunity for
practicing companionship, building relationships, eroding
boundaries, interrogating injustice, practicing tolerance, and
exhibiting Christ-like behavior. Burkhart noted that sharing a
meal in recognition of Christ provides a way for people to taste
the future to which they are being drawn. In this view, people
"who eat together are, like it or not, somehow bound
together."[20]

Prayer

Prayer is a conversation with God. It presupposes a belief in the personality of God, God's ability, and willingness to interact with us, and God's control of all things, creatures, and their actions.[21] There is no one right way to pray. Our prayers don't need to be lengthy, creative, or dramatic. They don't need to follow a formula or script. They only need to be sincere. Matthew 6:5–8 cautions us about the use of empty phrases when we pray. Sometimes the simplest prayers say it all. Remember the "tax collector's prayer" from Luke 18:13 (NLT)? "But the tax collector stood at a distance and dared not even lift his eyes to heaven as he prayed. Instead, he beat his chest in sorrow, saying, 'O God, be merciful to me, for I am a sinner.'"

The New Testament says a lot about prayer. The Apostle Paul instructed that we should pray in the Spirit on all occasions with all kinds of prayers and requests (Ephesians 6:18). In his letter to the Philippians, Paul reminds us that we should "be careful about nothing; but in everything by prayer and supplication with thanksgiving let your requests be made known unto God" (Philippians 4:6). He tells the church at Thessalonica to pray without ceasing (1 Thessalonians 5:17). Scripture also tells us that effectual and fervent prayers are powerful; through them, we can be healed (James 5:15-16).

From a practical standpoint, prayer allows us to let go of our anger, frustration, bitterness, resentment, or whatever negative energy we are harboring. As we release that energy in prayer, God restores us and gives us new reasons to hope. The more we ask, the more God gives. God changes our minds and our hearts. Through prayer, God makes us whole and gives us peace. All we have to do is ask for help.

Preaching - The Word of God

My current denomination, the United Church of Christ, embraces the Word of God as Scripture and acknowledges the presence and power of the Holy Spirit to further the church's redemptive work in the world. In other denominations with which I have been associated, congregants are encouraged to listen *to* the Word of God. In the UCC, congregants are directed to listen *for* the Word of God. Hence, the United Church of Christ promotes the position that "God is still speaking" through God's Holy Word.

Moreover, the United Church of Christ heeds the words and deeds of the prophets and apostles, thereby seeking discernment of standards for righteousness and justice. The church uses the Bible as a conceptual framework for present-day decision-making. Hence, for me and the United Church of Christ, the Bible is the living word.

As ministerial leaders, you may be called on to preach a sermon in your setting. You should consider these factors when you are preparing to preach. Although it is difficult to classify and categorize all sermon styles and types, most sermons fall into three categories: expository, textual, and topical.[22]

Expository. An expository sermon uses biblical text to form your theme, main point, and minor points. You may include biblical quotes throughout your expository sermon. Your main point should establish your theme, such as quoting from a biblical passage. Use your minor points to show instances in the Bible where these lessons are demonstrated, but keep your sermon focused on the biblical text.

Textual. Textual sermons use biblical text to form the main point and minor points of your sermon. However, you develop your theme based on a message that you believe your congregation needs to learn. Textual sermon outlines begin with a Biblical text and provide the overall subject or concept, and move into providing the main points of the sermon. All of the sub-points are left up to the preacher to determine as the preacher sees fit.

Topical. Topical sermons use biblical text to form the minor points of your sermon. You develop your themes and major points from your experience as a Christian and your general knowledge of the Bible. You should include both major and minor points from the Scripture to strengthen your topic. Topical sermon outlines begin with a Biblical concept or reference but are completely based upon the slant of the preacher.

Sermon Preparation

In a presentation called "Preaching Is Back in Style," Frank Thomas argues that one of the keys to profound preaching is structure.[23] He says the sermon is an audible movement of thought across time. The structure of a sermon should be smooth and efficient and should provide the logic and flow of the message. If the sermon is too slow, the people get bored and wander. If the sermon is too fast, people give up listening and wander.

One way to format the sermon is to use a four-step framework that includes a situation, complication, resolution, and celebration. Thomas uses this example: The situation might involve a boy asking his father for his inheritance. The complication explains what goes wrong with this picture – the boy ends up living a riotous life. The resolution comes with a report on the good news, which occurs when the boy goes back home to his father. The celebration provides an opportunity to rejoice in the good news that there's going to be a party in honor of the boy's return, and the son that was once lost is now found.

Now, you should practice crafting your own sermon. Using the following guidelines adapted from Frank Thomas,[24] begin to outline a sermon you would like to preach in your setting. You should start by selecting a text or passage from the Bible. Next, write a summary of the passage in one or two sentences. Ask these questions: (a) What does this passage say to me? (b) What does this passage say to the needs of the members in our time? (c) What is the "bad news" in the text? What is the "bad news" for our time? (d) What is the "good news" in the text? What is the "good news" for our time? After you've responded to the above question, you should start to focus on writing a behavioral purpose statement (for example, I propose:… At the end hearers will: …). Remember that your sermon will end with a celebration. So, the last thing you will do is write your strategy for celebration by responding to the following questions: (a) What shall we celebrate? (b) How shall we celebrate? (c) What materials of celebration shall we use?

You might find it helpful to edit your written draft a few times to make sure everything is the way you want it. It also helps if you practice your sermon and record your delivery. This gives you an opportunity to engage in self-critique. After that, all that's left is for you to trust your manuscript and rely on the Holy Spirit to do the rest.

Extravagant Welcome

Concerning the whole worship experience, I appreciate the position of the United Church of Christ as welcoming, affirming, and inclusive. I agree with the church that all people of faith are created in the image of God, regardless of race, class, sex, or gender orientation and that God loves each one of us unconditionally. With the guidance of the Holy Spirit, the church engages in covenant relationships with all people of faith who are baptized in Christ and are part of a spiritual family. I believe that the sacrament of Baptism initiates us into the spiritual family of God. And the sacrament of the Eucharist nourishes us and strengthens our connections to Christ and each other. Through the body of Christ, God calls us to promote peace, speak truth to power, liberate the oppressed, care for the poor and comfort those who are troubled. Worship provides a way to reinforce these values.

The Liturgical Year

Seasonal services of the liturgical year include Advent, Christmas, Epiphany, Lent (beginning with Ash Wednesday), Holy Week (including Palm Sunday, Maundy Thursday, Good

Friday), Easter, and Pentecost. The Church uses particular colors during each season:

- **Violet**: Violet or purple is used during the seasons of Advent and Lent and may also be worn for funeral services.
- **White**: White is used for Easter and Christmas, Epiphany.
- **Red**: On Palm Sunday, Good Friday, and Pentecost Sunday, red is worn.
- **Green**: Green is worn during Ordinary Time.

THE INFLUENCE OF CULTURE ON WORSHIP

I've been fortunate enough to attend a variety of churches in my time – white, black, rich, poor, conservative, and liberal of various denominations. And I have observed differences in their worship styles. A few years ago, I began to reflect on these differences as I thought about a statement the Rev. Dr. Martin Luther King, Jr., made decades ago: He said, "it is appalling that the most segregated hour of Christian America is eleven o'clock on Sunday morning."[25] During one of my seminary experiences, I began to explore this assertion and concluded that real differences exist between black and white ways of worshiping. Many of them are related to cultural preferences. In this section, I will share with you a couple of examples of what I've seen.

Worship Experience – A

I attended a worship service at one of my former seminaries a few years ago during Holy Week. It was intellectually stimulating. But at the same time, the preacher attempted to organize his ideas into taxonomies, ologies, and isms. The litany consisted of a highly scripted call-and-response. There was no room for spontaneity. During the sermon, the preacher quoted scholars and highlighted the political aspects of Jesus's ministry. He was focused on his perception that Jesus's actions were radical and subversive. The congregation sang songs of justice and their noble obligation to help the poor. For this is what scripture tells us, isn't it?

Worship Experience – B

For a long time, I defined "church" in terms of experiences from my youth. The church was a family affair. Everybody served; no one just watched. The sermons consisted of vivid examples of the gospel for daily living. Great care was taken to read the KJV scripture for the benefit of those in the congregation who could not read it for themselves. There was a pattern to the preaching. Scripture reading, explanation of the scripture, application of the scripture reduced to three major points the members could remember when they got home from church, and a celebration of all the ways that God has blessed us. The sermons typically reminded us that if God delivered God's chosen people out of bondage, God would surely deliver us, for we, too, were chosen. The music consisted mostly of songs about our struggles to survive and make it in a hostile world. Grace, mercy, faithfulness, healing were major themes of many songs we sang on a Sunday morning. And often our gratitude was accompanied by shouting, handclapping, and dancing. Quite a few of the songs identified with Jesus, our Redeemer who had suffered, bled, and died for us. Jesus was acquainted with our sorrow and our pain. He could relate to the misery we have endured, for he had endured some of the same degradations.

Worship Experience – C

One year in one of my seminary classes, the professor came up with the idea that we would wash each other's feet, as Jesus did for his disciples. So, we drew names from a hat. I ended up being paired with an older white male whose experiences with other cultures were limited, to say the least. When I thought about the act of kneeling at this white man's feet and washing them, I was overwhelmed with thoughts of my foremothers, bending, and bowing and kneeling before their slave master. In the days of chattel slavery, he cracked the whip, and they did his bidding so they could survive. I declined to participate in the exercise that day. But I readily shared my thoughts with the instructor and my classmates so they would understand my point of view. They had never thought of it like that before.

On a different occasion, I participated in a foot-washing ceremony at my home church. In the company of members who shared trust and a common consciousness, it was a moving and spiritual experience to be able to perform this selfless act. It was like embracing the wounds of a fellow traveler and letting them know that we were all in this together, no matter what. There was empathy and compassion and power in what we were doing for each other.

Different Songs We Sing

My last example comes from an experience I had at the Pentecostal church I attended before going to seminary. It was a good Friday service. The music alone stirred my soul. Oh, the blood of Jesus, the choir sang. When Resurrection Sunday came, we rejoiced because we are people of the resurrection, for Jesus got up! The music that day lifted our spirits and filled us with joy.

WORKSHOP EXERCISES

8:30 a.m. – 9:00 a.m.	Invocation/Welcome Introductions/Community Building Creating a Hospitable Environment
9:00 a.m. – 12:00 noon	**Workshop Session 1** **Activity 1 – Personal Experience** **Activity 2 – Questions on Worship**
12:30 p.m. – 1:00 p.m.	Lunch
2:00 p.m. – 5:00 p.m.	**Workshop Session 2** **Activity 1 – Variability in Church** **Activity 2 – Planning Worship**
5:30 p.m. – 6:00 p.m.	Workshop Evaluation Closing Worship, Benediction, Dismissal

Personal Experience: Think about your unique setting. Briefly describe an experience you had in preparing for or participating in worship. What was rewarding about the experience? What was challenging?

Questions on Worship
1. Discuss your thoughts on "one-size-fits-all" worship practices.
2. Identify the ways that culture influences your worship practices?
3. How can worship services be structured in a way that values the uniqueness of each individual?

Variability in Church: With a partner or in a group, read "Variability in Church Practices" and reflect on its content.

Variability in Church Practices

- I was hungry and you formed a humanities club and discussed my hunger.
- I was imprisoned and you crept off quietly to your chapel and prayed for my release.
- I was naked and, in your mind, you debated the morality of my appearance.
- I was sick and you knelt and thanked God for your health.
- I was homeless and you preached to me of the spiritual shelter of the love of God.
- I was lonely and you left me alone to go and pray for me.
- You seem so holy, so close to God.
- But I'm still very hungry and lonely and cold.

Author unknown.

Planning Worship: Plan a worship experience for a special occasion in your congregational setting.

SUGGESTED RESOURCES

"Worship Ways." Available at: https://www.ucc.org/what-we-do/justice-local-church-ministries/local-church/worship-resources/worship-ways-2/

"Sermon Seeds." Available at: https://www.ucc.org/what-we-believe/worship/sermon-seeds/

"Worship Resources." The Presbyterian Church (USA) provides a list of helpful worship resources. Available at https://www.pcusa.org/pcusa-worship-resources/

Chapter 5: Caring for Self and Others

CHAPTER PREVIEW

Readings and exercises in this chapter will help you:

- Assess situations and relationships with sensitivity to culture and context.
- Recognize sound spiritual counsel to those facing life transitions and end of life.
- Practice sensitivity to those making difficult decisions around major life events.
- Identify resources for your personal and professional wellness.

MAINTAINING WELLNESS – PASTORAL CARE

Some of the first questions you may be asking are, What is a caregiver? And what is pastoral care? Clinebell noted that caregivers are "called to facilitate healing of brokenness, not only with those who are like themselves but also with marginalized persons and groups."[26] Pastoral caregivers address the whole person in and outside of their faith communities. This requires flexibility and the ability to nurture the development of mind, body, and spirit. Pastoral care comprises all the techniques caregivers use to meet the emotional, social and spiritual needs of people from a variety of cultures and traditions.

Biblical Basis for Pastoral Care

One way to think about pastoral care is to develop what Clinebell calls "a working theology of caregiving." He places Christ at the center of a paradigm that emphasizes healing, wholeness, interdependency, and spiritual empowerment, thus "enabling members to deal with their violence, brokenness, destructiveness, and sinfulness."[27] Wholeness involves the unity of persons – bodies, minds, and spirits. In working out your theology of caregiving, you might find it helpful to start with the Bible.

Scriptures Related to Pastoral Care

As you have studied the Bible, you have probably noted that particular scriptures speak more vividly than others to your worldview and personal experiences in caregiving. In this section, I have provided several biblical sources that may influence your understanding of pastoral care. You should feel free to interject your favorites as you read through the section.

Disciples – The Great Commission (Matthew 28:18-20, NRSV) [18] And Jesus came and said to them, "All authority in heaven and on earth has been given to me. [19] Go therefore and make disciples of all nations, baptizing them in the name of the Father and of the Son and the Holy Spirit, [20] and teaching them to obey everything that I have commanded you. And remember, I am with you always, to the end of the age."

Caregivers – Feed My Sheep (John 21:15-17, NRSV) [15] When they had finished breakfast, Jesus said to Simon Peter, "Simon son of John, do you love me more than these?" He said to him, "Yes, Lord; you know that I love you." Jesus said to him, "Feed my lambs." [16] A second time he said to him, "Simon son of John, do you love me?" He said to him, "Yes, Lord; you know that I love you." Jesus said to him, "Tend my sheep." [17] He said to him the third time, "Simon son of John, do you love me?" Peter felt hurt because he said to him the third time, "Do you love me?" And he said to him, "Lord, you know everything; you know that I love you." Jesus said to him, "Feed my sheep.

Love - Loving One's Neighbor (Matthew 22:36-40, NRSV) [36] "Teacher, which commandment in the law is the greatest?" [37] He said to him, "'You shall love the Lord your God with all your heart, and with all your soul, and with all your mind.' [38] This is the greatest and first commandment. [39] And a second is like it: 'You shall love your neighbor as yourself.' [40] On these two commandments hang all the law and the prophets."

Togetherness - Living in Community (Acts 2:42-27, NLT) [42] All the believers devoted themselves to the apostles' teaching, and fellowship, and to sharing in meals (including the Lord's Supper), and to prayer. ... [46] They worshiped together at the Temple each day, met in homes for the Lord's Supper and shared their meals with great joy and generosity— [47] all the while praising God and enjoying the goodwill of all the people. And each day the Lord added to their fellowship those who were being saved.

Providing - Caring for Each Other (Matthew 25:35-36, NLT) [35] For I was hungry, and you fed me. I was thirsty, and you gave me a drink. I was a stranger, and you invited me into your home. [36] I was naked, and you gave me clothing. I was sick, and you cared for me. I was in prison, and you visited me.'

Compassion - Empathizing with Others (Romans 12:15-16, NJKV) "Rejoice with those who rejoice, and weep with those who weep. Agree with one another. Do not set your mind on high things, but associate with the humble. Do not be wise in your own opinion."

Forgiving - Showing Mercy to Each Other (Luke 17:3-4, NLT) [3] So watch yourselves! "If another believer sins, rebuke that person; then if there is repentance, forgive. [4] Even if that person wrongs you seven times a day and each time turns again and asks forgiveness, you must forgive."

Mutual Respect - Treating Others as We Want to Be Treated (Luke 6:27-31, NKJV) [27] "But I say to you who hear:

Love your enemies, do good to those who hate you, [28] bless those who curse you, and pray for those who spitefully use you. [29] To him who strikes you on the one cheek, offer the other also. And from him who takes away your cloak, do not withhold your tunic either. [30] Give to everyone who asks of you. And from him who takes away your goods do not ask them back. [31] And just as you want men to do to you, you also do to them likewise.

Compassion - <u>Helping Others to Rise and Walk</u> (Acts 3:2-6, NKJV) And a certain man lame from his mother's womb was carried, whom they laid daily at the gate of the temple, which is called Beautiful, to ask alms from those who entered the temple, who, seeing Peter and John about to go into the temple, asked for alms. And fixing his eyes on him, with John, Peter said, "Look at us." So, he gave them his attention, expecting to receive something from them. Then Peter said, "Silver and gold I do not have, but what I do have I give you: In the name of Jesus Christ of Nazareth, rise up and walk."

Shepherding - <u>Leaving No One Behind</u> - Parable of the Lost Sheep (Matthew 18:12, NLT) [12] "If a man has a hundred sheep and one of them wanders away, what will he do? Won't he leave the ninety-nine others on the hills and go out to search for the one that is lost?

Resiliency – <u>Enduring to the End</u> (Matthew 24:12-13, NRSV) [12] *And because of the increase of lawlessness, the love of many will grow cold.* [13] *But the one who endures to the end will be saved.*

Resiliency Theory in Action

You probably noticed that promoting resiliency is a common thread in the passages above. Resiliency is defined as the ability to cope or "bounce back" from adverse situations or stresses.[28] It can be viewed as the capacity to adapt successfully "despite exposure to severe stress…that is inherent in today's world."[29] Resiliency is innate within all of us.[30] Sometimes members need a bit of prompting to bring it to the surface.

Three protective factors contribute to resiliency. These factors include caring relationships, high expectations, and opportunities for meaningful participation/contribution in a caring community. These are also things Jesus taught us during his earthly ministry and preached about on several occasions.

Skills and Dispositions You Already Possess for Pastoral Care

What skills do you already possess for pastoral care? By heightening your awareness of your strengths and limitations, you will be less likely to let them interfere with your ability to minister to the needs of those who seek your help. Some areas of pastoral ministry may prove to be more difficult for you than others. Identifying those areas will alert you to the need for additional training and education or to areas you may need to avoid. It might also help to identify qualities and characteristics you already have for this kind of work. Let me use myself as an example of skills and dispositions I already possessed for pastoral care.

When I answered the call to ministry, I also discerned that a burden of compassion had been placed on my heart. Suddenly, my eyes were wide opened to the suffering of my sisters and brothers at the margins. I became aware that I was righteously angry, not only for myself but also for others. My anger emanated from society's insistence that I stay in the place that racism, sexism, and classism had assigned to members like me. At the same time, my burden of compassion dictated that I intervene in the cycle that was destroying my companions. In the next few paragraphs, I will share how I dealt with some of the challenges I faced.

Early in my career, I participated in an activity called the "privilege walk." [31] Participants were asked to form a straight line across the room about an arm's length apart and to leave space in front and behind. They were then asked to listen to several statements, such as "If you have blue eyes, take one step forward," only people with blue eyes would move and everyone else should stand still. As predicted, members of color were left behind at the starting lines.

It has been said that a chain is only as strong as its weakest link. Therefore, I used the insights from this activity to guide hurting people to resources that will strengthen them individually and, thereby, strengthen the chain overall. I am committed to helping those I serve to flip the narrative as it relates to marginalized people and racial minorities. Moreover, I actively facilitate the growth of my companions so they will learn how to help each other move forward with support and encouragement. From a biblical standpoint, I try to help them find ways that we must support each other so that all of us can endure to the end (Matthew 24:12-13).

During my ministerial training in seminary, I became aware of the devastating impact of domestic violence in the lives of women and men from all walks of life. My empathy flowed from my experiences as a child who grew up in a home where domestic abuse prevailed. I guess I was on a crusade back then because I tried to learn everything I could about the causes, impacts, and remedies of this devastating social ill. What I learned has helped me deal more sensitively with abuse victims. I passed my insights along to those in need of this information.

Additionally, I served for a while as a rape victim advocate. As such, I met young women in the emergency rooms of hospitals in the wee hours of the morning. There, I informed them of their rights to be treated justly. I listened and was present with them. I prayed with them and for them. In short, I did my best to empower them so they could heal and move forward after the devastation.

I've also been blessed to be an encouraging influence for members in various settings over time. These settings include my work as an educator, administrator, and minister. I am still amazed that God called me out of a career as a tenured university research professor into a life of service through

Christian ministry. One of my past responsibilities was to mentor students and facilitate the development of their dissertations. In both of these roles, I was a helper, a gentle critic, a sympathetic ear, a coach, and a cheerleader – all at the same time. You would be surprised at the number of students who were just about ready to throw in the towel; then, with a little encouragement and support, they persevered and finally achieved their goals.

My same penchant for facilitation and empathy showed up on many occasions during my time as an administrator. When students were sent to the principal's office, for example, I attempted to stimulate their critical thinking and problem-solving skills. At the same time, when students were treated unfairly, I championed their cause. I've always been an advocate for restorative justice.

Caregiving as a minister in the church where I recently served as associate pastor came naturally to me. I was in charge of Christian education and developed courses that allowed adults to engage in problem-solving as a group. In addition to the curriculum development and teaching, I was invited to gather with the ministers, deacons, seminarians, and worship leaders once a month to discuss issues in a "book talk" forum. We took turns, respected boundaries, and learned to disagree without being disagreeable – all valuable skills for caregiving.

My current church is small, so often after service many of us stick around to chat. This opens the door to being present, listening, praying, and recommending resources to address issues of concern. From time to time, parishioners have approached me asking for personal advice. Rather than tell them what to do outright, we have explored possibilities and options in a "what if" discussion. Our parishioners are like family members, and we do whatever we can to support each other. Laughter, festivities revolving around shared meals, participation in a community pantry, working together to give back to the community – all of these represent opportunities to express our compassion and care for one another.

Areas of Pastoral Care that Are Hardest For You

There will be occasions when caregiving does not come easy for you. Again, I will share with you some of my personal experiences I found to be challenging. One of those was watching a family member succumb to Alzheimer's. Over a few years, I saw my father-in-law regress from a vibrant, opinionated, and amusingly obstreperous man to one who did not remember our names when we came to visit with him in the nursing home. For some reason, my husband and many family members leaned on me for support, consolation, and decision making, as if I was the strong one. The skills I acquired during this phase of my life have been invaluable as I continue to give care to others in similar situations.

Another difficult caregiving experience occurred when I was a hospital chaplain intern. I had to be ready for anything. For example, one nephew rudely told me that his uncle didn't need my services. A few days later, the uncle passed away. The nephew approached me with remorse and apologized for the way he had spoken to me. He wished that he had not interfered. I assured him that I was not offended and accepted his apology. He thanked me for being patient and for any spiritual relief I may have provided for his uncle.

I completed one of my CPEs in a hospice center. We were assigned to teams that included a social worker, primary care physician, registered nurse, certified nurse assistant, and chaplain. As the chaplain intern at that time, I was responsible for ministering to the needs of the members of our caseload. We visited clients in nursing homes, hospitals, and their places of residence. Each situation was different. I had to be prepared to meet members wherever they were emotionally and spiritually on the day of my visit. I encountered wide ranges in the moods, physical conditions, and the capacities of my clients to communicate. Staying on my toes was essential.

I remember one patient who was actively dying. I provided support for him as well as for his family. I ended up putting the family in contact with a social worker and a funeral home that would be able to cremate the loved one. For the patient who was dying, I sat beside his bed and read to him from the Bible for hours. The nurses had told me that hearing was the last thing to go, so, I trusted that this patient received comfort from my efforts. There are many other stories I could tell. I can say that the hospice experience challenged me in many areas but blessed me in many others.

I've enjoyed an amazing range of opportunities to be helpful. But I don't feel equipped or prepared to do a good job in all of them. Without a doubt, hospice care was the hardest for me. At the same time, it was my privilege to accompany members as they made their transitions to the next stage of being. It was a precious and awesome responsibility, which I did not take lightly. On the other hand, hospital caregiving was hard in a different way. Some hospital campuses are expansive, and I had difficulty doing all the walking and climbing that was required in some cases. Hospital and hospice care are two vocational areas I would avoid in the future. However, I am willing to consider all other options.

Self-care is Critical

As you engage in pastoral care, you might find the experience to be emotionally, physically, and spiritually draining at times. When you start to feel depleted, you must find ways to replenish yourself. I will close this section by describing what I have done to take care of myself. Journaling has been my lifeline. I've spent several hours a day committing my doodles, thoughts, feelings, and prayers to paper. During one of my internships, I wrote over 125 poems, as I used poetry writing as a reflective tool. Frequently, I spoke to supporters whom I believed could encourage me on my journey. For example, I met often with the associate pastor from the church I belonged to at the time. I've even sought advice and care from professional counselors and therapists to help me process my experiences. As another coping mechanism, I've cherished my solitude and quietude when I've needed to regroup. All these mechanisms have been enormously helpful. In conclusion, as part of this sacred calling to accompany members who are challenged by their circumstances, I realize that I don't have all the answers. But I know how to be present for them and direct them to resources that may be helpful.

Self-care Covenant

Not too long ago, I developed a covenant with myself to attend to my personal, intellectual, and spiritual needs. I consider this covenant to be a solemn agreement to attend to my own well-being. You may have other needs, but when I wrote the covenant, these were my major priorities. Use the covenant below as a model for writing your own.

My Covenant with Self

I, _____ enter into this covenant with self to ensure my ongoing well-being as I engage in the pastoral care of others. I covenant to do the following:

Organizational Commitments

- Complete Ministerial Ethics training (Boundaries) provided by the United Church of Christ every three years in order to maintain my standing in the denomination.
- Maintain a reasonable schedule for completing work assignments.
- Say "no" if I feel I do not have the resources (time, patience, expertise, etc.) to carry out an assignment effectively.

Mental

- Reading – engage in reading for inspiration, professional development, and entertainment.
- Journaling – make weekly entries in my journal.
- Guard my peace – distance myself from things that "disturb my peace."
- Silence – use silence as a way of relaxing my mind.

My Covenant (continued)

Physical
- Sleep – get at least 8 hours of sleep each night.
- Exercise – engage in physical exercise at least twice a week.
- In-house spa – use aromatherapy, sauna, and warm baths as forms of relaxation.
- Diet – maintain a healthy diet by adhering to the parameters of my current regimen.
- Breathing – practice deep breathing as a form of relaxation.

Spiritual
- Meditation/devotion – engage in daily meditation and devotional reading.
- Music – use relaxing music as a form of spiritual gratification.
- Sabbath – honor my commitment to maintain at least one work-free day each week.
- Prayer – engage in pray daily.

Social
- Movies – attend/view movies with family as a form of entertainment.
- Family outings – host and attend family gatherings on a range of occasions.
- Date nights – coordinate with my husband for periodic getaways.

Signature: _____

Date: _____

WORKSHOP EXERCISES

8:30 a.m. – 9:00 a.m.	Invocation/Welcome Introductions/Community Building Creating a Hospitable Environment
9:00 a.m. – 12:00 noon	**Workshop Session 1** **Activity 1 – Dispositions Exercise** **Activity 2 – Case Analysis**
12:30 p.m. – 1:00 p.m.	Lunch
2:00 p.m. – 5:00 p.m.	**Workshop Session 2** **Activity 1 – Case Analysis** **Activity 2 – Self-care Covenant**
5:30 p.m. – 6:00 p.m.	Workshop Evaluation Closing Worship, Benediction, Dismissal

Learning Activity: Dispositions

- Think about your previous work experiences. Make a list of skills and dispositions you already possess for pastoral care.
- Again, given your past work experiences, make a list your dispositions and attitudes that might interfere with your effectiveness as a pastoral caregiver.

Personal Experience: Recall a time when you were in a position to help a person in need. Describe how you felt. What would you do differently if faced with the same situation again?

Personal Experience: Now think about your unique setting. Briefly describe an experience you had in caring for self or others. What was rewarding about the experience? What was challenging?

Self-care Covenant: Write a covenant for your self-care. Include commitments for professional, mental, physical, spiritual, and social areas of your life. Be as through as you can, and remember to sign the document at the end.

Case Analysis
Cases in this chapter are based on experiences I had during my chaplain internships and CPE. Imagine that you are in these situations. What are your reactions to the scenarios presented? How would you handle the situations differently in your setting?

Case 1: Vent Removal
Over the past week, Andrew's condition had steadily declined. His interdisciplinary care team met with his mother to discuss her son's options. The team consisted of the administrative manager, the attending physician, the nurse and CNA, the social worker, and the hospital chaplain. Each member of the team served a particular role. The manager coordinated the whole operation, making sure that weekly meetings occurred regularly and that HIPAA rules were followed. The manager also took responsibility for completing the paperwork and making sure that decisions were communicated to appropriate individuals in a reasonable amount of time. The attending physician conferred with the team on matters about pain management and medical care.

The nurses and CNAs performed a critical function. They attended to the patient's day-to-day physical and emotional care. They were involved with the most intimate aspects of his well-being. They were responsible for giving baths, skin and mouth care, feeding, and toileting. They also did light housekeeping and ran errands if that's what the circumstances demanded at the time. The social worker was responsible for providing emotional support and arranging for community resources, financial assistance, if necessary, transportation, and government benefits. The chaplain offered spiritual support to the patient and the family.

After reviewing Andrew's history and the circumstances of his case, the team laid out the pros and cons of removing Andrew from his ventilator. As the person with Andrew's medical power of attorney, his mother supported the idea. And the vent removal was scheduled to take place on Friday afternoon.

The ritual was to be a formal litany, complete with assigned speeches and choral responses. The hospital chaplain handed Andrew's family members copies of the ceremonial document. When everyone was present, they were escorted to the "living room" where they talked about Andrew's life and antics. In round-robin fashion, old classmates and neighbors recalled their fondest memories of Andrew.

After the period of reminiscence, the chaplain explained to the family what the vent removal procedure would entail and took a few minutes to examine the litany he had distributed. As everyone read through the ceremony, various members volunteered to take responsibility for certain parts of it. Then the chaplain left the room briefly to get his Bible, which he had left on his desk. When he returned, Andrew's mother began to speak quietly.

"You know what?" she said. "We're non-denominational. Couldn't we just say a prayer or something?"

Without hesitation, the chaplain said, "Absolutely." When the time came, Andrew's primary nurse notified everyone that the respiratory therapist had arrived. The nurse escorted the group to the room, where the therapist had already begun her work. As the respiratory therapist continued, the nurse again explained each step in the procedure. She told the family that their prayer should be that Andrew would breathe on his own after the machinery was disconnected.

The vent was removed, and Andrew began to breathe without assistance.

"Everything is in God's hands now," Andrew's mother announced.

A few seconds had passed, the chaplain read two scriptures he had selected for the occasion. Everyone in the room joined hands around Andrew's bed, as he prayed. He thanked God for Andrew's life. He asked God to be with Andrew on the last few steps of his journey on this side of life. He told God that none of us understands death; it frightens us and intrigues us at the same time. But be that as it may, we were putting our trust in God.

The chaplain asked God to give the family comfort and strength and to show them ways to fill the empty places that would grow in their spirits in the days to come. He asked God to give them courage and compassion to forgive the ones who had hurt them. He asked God to help everyone remember that God is faithful and is still in control. Finally, he asked God to help everyone remember that absolutely nothing could separate us from God's everlasting love.

"Amen." He spoke.

"Amen." The others repeated.

Case Study Analysis Guidelines

1. What are the presenting problems as they relate to the topic of pastoral and self-care? Define the nature of the problem(s).
2. Using relevant details from the case, identify the deeper issues if any. Evaluate the seriousness of the issues.
3. Reflect theologically on the issue(s) you identified?
4. Determine the extent to which some kind of action is required immediately.
5. Identify two or more alternative solutions based on your analysis and theological reflection.
6. Describe a plan to implement your solution.

Case 2: Bereavement Visit

On the day of Andrew's funeral, Carrie Mae came bearing gifts. She placed the pound cake on the counter in the kitchen, which was abuzz with activity. The bereavement ministry was busy heating fried chicken and greens and macaroni and cheese they had prepared and brought over for the family and friends. Three or four of the deacons from Calvary had stopped by to console Joyce Johnson, Andrew's mother. Quite a few of Andrew's friends had also paid their respects. Carrie Mae recognized some of the young men and women. Three or four of them were on Jefferson's basketball team. They stood together in the corner of the living room and remained quiet, as the young men held their skullcaps in their hands and bowed their heads in reverence. They declined the offer of food. After about a half-hour, they left as a group, each of them passing by Andrew's mother and offering condolences. Joyce Johnson seemed to appreciate that her son's friends had stopped by to visit. It showed that they still cared about life, in her opinion. Over the years, Joyce Johnson had learned a lot about life and death.

The living room was empty now, except for Carrie Mae and Joyce who sat beside each other on the sofa.

"I am so sorry for your loss," Carrie Mae said.

"Andrew was trying to do something positive with his life. He wasn't like all the rest of those thugs out there. He was in activities at school. He was involved in the student council. He was making good grades. I just can't understand why this would happen to him. Andrew was my only living child. You may or may not know that I had four children. Now I have none. My daughter was shot and killed at age 15 while she was on her way to the library. Andrew's brothers were gunshot victims, too. His brother Chris died when he was only 18 years old. He was arguing with another boy over some gym shoes and the boy pulled out a gun and shot him. Then there was Andrew's brother Tommy. Somebody killed Tommy when he was 23. He was standing at a payphone when a van pulled up, and someone opened fire. It was mistaken identity, they said."

Carrie Mae sat closer to Joyce.

"This is crazy," Joyce said. "I never thought I'd be burying all my children before I died. That goes against the natural order of things. You can't even imagine what it's like to lose a child — let alone all your kids."

Carrie Mae had no words to say. How could she console this grieving mother? She was tempted to tell Joyce not to cry because God's plan was beyond understanding. She was very close to telling Joyce that weeping endures for only a night, but joy comes in the morning. Perhaps, now was not the right time to say that Jesus's love has conquered death. In her present state of mind, Joyce was not ready to hear any of it.

"This killing has got to stop," Joyce whispered after several minutes. "You never get over it, you know. The death of a child. No matter what else happens, you'll love that child forever. I still love every one of my four children, as if they were still here with me. Love never dies. And because of that, the grief never dies. The emptiness never goes away. It's especially painful during holidays and special occasions that your kids should be celebrating. Like birthdays. Or graduations. Or Christmas."

"I can only imagine," said Carrie Mae. Deep in her spirit, she knew that she should say nothing. So, the two women sat silently for a long time.

Case Study Analysis Guidelines
1. What are the presenting problems as they relate to the topic of pastoral and self-care? Define the nature of the problem(s).
2. Using relevant details from the case, identify the deeper issues if any. Evaluate the seriousness of the issues.
3. Reflect theologically on the issue(s) you identified?
4. Determine the extent to which some kind of action is required immediately.
5. Identify two or more alternative solutions based on your analysis and theological reflection.
6. Describe a plan to implement your solution.

SUGGESTED RESOURCES

"Faithfully Facing Dying: A Lenten Study Guide on Critical Issues and Decisions for the Members of the United Church of Christ." Available at:
https://www.ucc.org/what-we-do/justice-local-church-ministries/justice/health-and-wholeness-advocacy-ministries/health-care-justice/faithfully_facing_dying/

"Recovering Hope" Available at:
https://www.ucc.org/disaster_index/recovering_hope/

"134 Activities to Add to Your Self-Care Plan," Available at:
https://www.goodtherapy.org/blog/134-activities-to-add-to-your-self-care-plan/

Chapter 6: Teaching and Learning

CHAPTER PREVIEW

Readings and exercises in this chapter will help you:
- Show competency in teaching in ministerial settings.
- Serve as an educator and advocate in an area of social justice work.
- Develop a curriculum and evaluate its effectiveness.

CURRICULUM DEVELOPMENT

Every good Bible study begins with a *curriculum*, which is defined as a set of planned and objective conditions specifying the interactions that will occur between teacher and student. Curriculum planning is just as important for Christian education as it is for other forums where teaching and learning take place. Many models for curriculum development exist. Ralph Tyler[32] was influential in defining what are now standard parameters for curriculum development. Tyler's basic questions are still in use to provide direction for curriculum projects:

1. What educational purposes should you seek to attain?
2. What educational experiences can be provided that are likely to attain these purposes?
3. How can these educational experiences be effectively organized?
4. How can we determine whether these purposes are being attained?

Tyler also believed that the curriculum should take into account (a) the nature of the learner (developmental factors, learner interests, and needs, life experiences, etc.); (b) the values and aims of society (democratizing principles, values, and attitudes); and (c) knowledge of subject matter (what is believed to be worthy and usable knowledge).

THE ART AND CRAFT OF TEACHING

Adult Learners

With a well-planned curriculum in hand, educators should be prepared to facilitate learning that is sensitive to the ways that adults learn. Christian educators responsible for teaching adults should focus on solving problems, honoring life experiences, providing information, raising self-esteem, developing support networks, and facilitating spiritual well-being. Unfortunately, most Bible study curricula do not cater to these needs. On the contrary, typical Bible study curricula I have observed often focus on literal understanding, rote memorization, or lower-level cognitive skills. Learners who are involved in these types of curricula may feel a high level of comfort with their ability to recite chapter and verse, but they may be less comfortable when it comes to applying what they have learned to the dynamic and often perplexing situations they encounter in life.

Adults bring to the learning arena previous life experience, a broad knowledge base, as well as professional and social competencies. Therefore, your lessons should include opportunities for the mature learner to experience the immediate application of the knowledge they are consuming. The lessons you plan should approach the learning task from a problem-centered perspective that emphasizes grappling with new information and looking at old knowledge with fresh eyes and personal insights.

Constructivism

Adult learners respond well to a curriculum based on the conceptual paradigm of *constructivism*, in which learners create personal meaning from shared information. Constructivism, according to Brooks and Brooks, is a:

> *"theory about knowledge and learning. Drawing on a synthesis of current work in cognitive psychology, philosophy, and anthropology, the theory defines knowledge as temporary, developmental, socially, and culturally mediated, and thus, non-objective. Learning from this perspective is understood as a self-regulated process of resolving inner cognitive conflicts that often become apparent through concrete experience, collaborative discourse, and reflection."[33]*

Stated in another way, constructivists view learning not as the passive reception of information but as active engagement in a process that accounts for the social context from which the information is taken. In that regard, knowledge is socially constructed and grows out of the understanding of each learner.

Critical Consciousness

Critical consciousness is another higher-order process you should be aware of when you are planning lessons for adults.[34] This reflective process requires learners to think critically and encourages them to find the hidden meaning in underlying assumptions. It entails "learning to see, in the mundane particulars of ordinary lives, how history works, how received ways of thinking and feeling serve to perpetuate existing structures of inequality."[35]

Paulo Freire[36] developed the concept of critical consciousness in Brazil. There, Freire observed that oppression was reflected in both high rates of functional illiteracy and a lack of critical literacy to "read" social conditions that perpetuate injustice and marginalization among the oppressed. Such conditions include the inequitable distribution of resources and access to opportunity. To combat this, Freire developed a pedagogical method focused upon reflection and analysis of the sociopolitical environment (critical literacy) and then acting upon it. This capacity for critical reflection and critical action was called "critical consciousness." Research shows that critical consciousness can be used to challenge racism, sexism, and other forms of social injustice.

Racial Justice as a Topic For Reflection and Lesson Planning

Leaders in today's church frequently have to confront sensitive topics such as environmental injustice, gay marriage, gun violence, economic inequity, and other topics that may be outside the scope of the ministerial leader's experience. One of those topics is racial justice, which is a systemic problem. Systemic racism includes the policies and practices entrenched in organizations, and it manifests in the exclusion or promotion of designated groups. Voices contributing to debates about race and racism are diverse, yet they often clash on major issues. As congregations grapple with racial justice, it is important for the ministerial leader to have awareness of racialized realities of the day.

Understanding the powerful, yet insidious, impact of racism in our lives, our communities, and our churches will require consideration of social, economic, and cultural factors. More importantly, for the ministerial leader, understanding will require deep introspection and insight from a theological perspective. What is God calling you to do with regard to racial injustice?

Exercises at the end of this chapter will help you plan a set of lessons to teach about racial justice. In your lessons, you should provide opportunities to describe the breadth and subtleties of racism and name examples of it within your communities and congregations. These exercises will guide you through reflection about the role of the church in confronting racial injustice.

Perspective Transformation

Perspective Transformation grows out of the work of John Mezirow,[37] who asserted that transformative learning occurs when a person undergoes a permanent change in the foundation of one's beliefs, values, commitments, and conduct.[38] Transformative learning is a theory of adult learning that seeks to explain the dramatic changes in worldview, paradigms, and "meaning perspectives" among various members. King noted that transformative learning theory uses a "disorienting dilemma" prompting adult learners to reexamine previously held values, assumptions, beliefs, and perspectives.[39] The discomfort of inner conflict, in turn, impels individuals to embark on a personal journey to make sense of their newly changed world.[40] Although transformative learning theory focuses on the individual, the model assumes that each person is a social being. Taylor stated that as learners move toward forging connections with others, "they learn to bring themselves fully into relationship and community while still maintaining their integrity as individuals" (p. 163). The processes described might lead to transformations in members' attitudes towards change, justice, resiliency, and self-efficacy.

The framework uses a "disorienting dilemma" to prompt adult learners to reexamine previously held values, assumptions, beliefs, and perspectives. The discomfort of inner conflict compels individuals on a personal journey to make sense of their newly changed world. This, in turn, prepares learners to become agents of change. Using the language of Thomas Kuhn,[41] transformative learning is similar to a "paradigm shift," or what occurs when a person undergoes a permanent change in the foundation of one's beliefs, values, commitments, and conduct.

Transformative learning in the context of systemic organizational change could facilitate modifications in religious organization cultures and climates. The modification would require adult learners to deconstruct rules, assumptions, and images; reflect on them; and reconstruct belief structures that enhance the social ecology. Mezirow's perspective transformation framework consists of phases, which are outlined in the paragraphs below.

Steps in the Perspective Transformation Process

Phase 1 - Identify the disorienting dilemma. This step typically results from the convergence of several "disquieting" events or experiences that tend to upset the equilibrium within the organization and its members. What are some of the major areas of concern presented in this case? Identify the most immediate areas of concern – the disorienting dilemmas. State the dilemma(s) in simple terms.

Phase 2 - Self-examination (Look). This phase involves deep introspection about the problems or situations. Engagement with this phase might entail members having critical conversations about the major issues. Questions that might facilitate organizational self-examination include: What are the major issues? How are they interconnected? In what ways do the organization's problems impede the accomplishment of your goal(s). What specific personnel or organizational adjustments will have to be made if the major issues are to be resolved?

Phase 3 - Critical analysis of assumptions (Think) This phase requires members to examine their assumptions about members, places, things, or circumstances that could inhibit or facilitate goal achievement. Such assumptions should be deconstructed, critically assessed, and reconstructed in ways that enable movement toward the desired goal. Questions include the following: Does everyone in the organization look at the issue in the same way? What are the points of departure and convergence? What are the likely sources (or root causes) of the problem? Respond to the following critical consciousness questions: How do we know what we know? Who's speaking? What causes what? How might things have been different? Who cares? What programs and policies need to be adjusted to support goal attainment?[42] Identify opportunities for all parties to participate in goal attainment.

Phase 4 - This phase assumes that the members' level of discontent with circumstances will serve as a motivator for change leading to transformation. Questions that might help to clarify the situation include: What prohibits the organization or community from reaching the desired goal? What would be the consequences if the desired change were not made?

Phase 5 - Exploration of options, including New roles, relationships, and actions. If change is warranted, members have to explore new roles, options, relationships, and actions, along with long-term and short-term implications.

Phase 6 - Planning a course of action (Act). Planning a new course of action entails developing a set of steps to move you closer to your goal. Guiding questions might include: What steps must be taken to reach your goal? What new roles and relationships should be cultivated to advance the movement toward the goal? What are other details that need to be considered in your action plan? (i.e., "who, what, when, where, why, and how").

Phase 7 - Acquiring knowledge and skills for implementing the plan This phase involves helping members acquire knowledge and skills needed to implement the action plan. This list of skill-building activities does not need to be all-inclusive but should provide members opportunities to build competence in critical areas. Questions to be addressed at this phase include: What are the organization's current strengths and weaknesses of goal achievement? What resources are accessible to help members build competence and self-confidence in their redefined roles and relationships?

Phase 8 - Provisional trying of new roles This phase involves members practicing acquired skills and acquiring experiences. Questions to be considered at this phase include: What new skills and knowledge have members acquired to nurture the goal? What lessons have members learned so far? What additional opportunities exist for growth and development?

Phase 9 - Building competence and self-confidence in new roles and relationships Building competence and self-confidence entail involvement in opportunities to improve performance in the new role(s). Develop a tentative list of possible opportunities for building competence and self-confidence. What are the costs involved in pursuing each opportunity?

Phase 10 - Reintegration into one's life of conditions dictated by one's new perspective For this phase, reintegration is defined as what occurs after the change has been completed. Questions include: In what ways are the members equipped to apply newfound skills and insights to achieving and sustaining the goal? In what ways should the organization invest materially, intellectually, physically, and emotionally to sustain the goal? What mechanisms will be used to engage in constant reflection and revision of the goal?

Forum for Theological Exploration (CARE)

The CARE model represents a teaching and problem-solving approach that invites people to think about and initiate profound change for their inner well-being as well as their communities of accountability. The CARE model includes four stages: **creating** a hospitable environment, **asking** self-awakening/ orienting questions, **reflecting theologically**, and **enacting** the next most faithful step. According to the model's developers, when the CARE model is contextualized creatively, the process helps people to discover "another way" of leading and the expanded capacity for facilitating sustainable change personally, communally, and globally. This model is adapted from *Another Way: Living and Leading Change on Purpose,*[43] a book that has its roots in the Forum for Theological Exploration

(FTE), a leadership incubator for the church and academy. The authors of the book state:

> *People who experience CARE-infused leadership sink into their honest selves and experience a mysterious relatedness among strangers. They come up out of a session led with CARE principles feeling changed, empowered, and able to take the next step. It is an effect at once deeply familiar and countercultural. It has a stickiness that reverberates in the communities to which people return. When we see it happening, we are reminded that people are built to experience community, to find joy in one another, and to create a better world out of a deep reservoir where the soul resides.* [44]

Using this approach, the process of teaching and learning tends to critique inherited ways of reading sacred literature and social life, thereby enabling participants to glimpse alternatives to the status quo, build experimental alternatives, or help change ineffective and unjust systems. This type of group reflection "dismantles the dominant forms of living and leading that reinforce the oppressive norms of empire."[45] With regular use, the practices begin to affect "building trust, creating circles of deep listening, asking a reflective question, and using silence, writings" and other reflections to evoke shared truth.

CONSTRUCTING LESSONS

Madeline Hunter Lesson Design

Regardless of the educational setting, all lessons should be based on a plan. An educator by the name of Madeline Hunter developed a strategy for planning lessons based on a seven-step lesson design. Steps in the model are shown below:

1 Anticipatory Set
2 Stating Lesson Objective
3 Instructional Input
4 Modeling

5 Checking for Understanding
6 Guided Practice
7 Independent Practice

Steps in Lesson Design

Unit Title/Lesson Title:
Objectives (Write 2-5 objectives stating expected learner outcomes.):
Materials/Resources Needed:
Anticipatory Set (List specific statements or activities you will use to focus students on the lesson for the day.):
Objective/Purpose (For the student's benefit, explain what students will be able to do by the end of the lesson and why these objectives are important to accomplish.):
Input (What information is essential for the student to know before beginning and how will this skill be communicated to students?):
Model (If you will be demonstrating the skill or competence, how will this be done?):
Check for Understanding (Identify strategies to be used to determine if students have learned the objectives.):
Guided Practice (List activities that will be used to guide student practice and provide a time frame for completing this practice.):
Closure (What method of review and evaluation will be used to complete the lesson?):
Independent Practice (List homework/seatwork assignment to be given to students to ensure they have mastered the skill without teacher guidance.):

Bloom's Taxonomy of the Educational Objectives

Every lesson should contain educational objectives. Bloom's Taxonomy of Educational Objectives is a system for classifying levels of learning when structuring lessons. Bloom said the objectives should be written with an audience, behavior, condition, and learning degree taken into consideration. These ideas are described here:

Audience: The audience to which objectives are written must always be the students (adult or otherwise). Example - The students will...

Behavior: Objectives must always describe the desired student behavior. Example – Match...

Conditions: Objectives must describe the conditions under which students are expected to perform the desired behavior. Example - Given a list of the atomic weights and symbols for 20 elements ...

Degree: Objectives must tell the degree of accuracy that is expected of students. Example - 80 percent accuracy.

Example of an Objective: By the end of this lesson, using life experiences, materials provided in this book as well as YouTube videos and other resources, adult learners will describe the breadth and subtleties of racism and name examples of it within their communities and congregations. Students will reflect on their insights after conferring with other learners in their group.

Levels of Bloom's Taxonomy

Educators have used Bloom's taxonomy to ensure that higher-order thinking is built into lessons. The following section provides examples of verbs you can use at each level of thinking. You may draw from the following list to state the nature of the learning that is to take place when you are constructing your objectives. Notice that the complexity of thinking increases as the levels increase on the taxonomy.

Knowledge

- Remembering previously learned material
- Recall of facts
- The lowest level of learning outcomes

Examples of Knowledge Verbs

- Knows common terms
- Identifies specific facts
- Describes methods and procedures
- States basic concepts
- Defines principles

Comprehension

- Ability to grasp the meaning of material
- Translating material from one form to another
- Explaining or summarizing material
- Predicting consequences or effects
- Goes one step beyond remembering material

Examples of Comprehension Verbs

- Understands facts and principles
- Interprets verbal material
- Interprets charts and graphs
- Translates verbal material to mathematical formats
- Estimates future consequences implied in data
- Justifies methods and procedures

Application

- Use learned material in new and concrete situations
- Apply rules, concepts, principles, and laws and theories
- Requires higher level of understanding than comprehension

Examples of Application Verbs

- Applies concepts and principles to new situations

- Applies laws and theories to practical situations
- Solves mathematical problems
- Constructs charts and graphs
- Demonstrates correct usage of a method or procedure

Analysis

- Break down the material into parts
- Identification of parts
- Analysis of relationship between parts
- Recognition of organizational principles
- Requires understanding of structural form

Examples of Analysis Verbs

- Recognizes unstated assumptions
- Recognizes logical fallacies in reasoning
- Distinguishes between facts and inferences
- Breaks down the organizational structure of works

Synthesis

- Put parts together to form a new whole
- Production of a unique communication
- Develop a research proposal
- Outcomes in this area are creative behaviors

Examples of Synthesis Verbs

- Write a well-organized theme
- Deliver a well-organized speech
- Write a creative short story
- Propose a plan for an experiment
- Integrate learning from different areas into a plan for solving problems
- Formulate a new classification scheme

Evaluation

- Judge the value of material
- Judgments based on criteria
- Contains elements of all other cognitive categories

Examples of Evaluation Verbs

- Judges the logical consistency of written material
- Judges the adequacy of conclusions
- Judges the value of work by use of internal criteria
- Judges the value of work by use of external criteria

Lesson Planning Using CARE and Madeline Hunter

CARE	Madeline Hunter
Creating a Hospitable Environment	Anticipatory Set Stating Objectives
Asking self-awakening/orienting questions	Instructional Input Modeling
Reflecting theologically	Checking for Understanding Guided Practice
Enacting the next most faithful step.	Independent Practice

Stages of CARE – Planning a Lesson on Racial Justice

Stages in CARE	Components of the Lesson
Creating a Hospitable Environment	Overview/Invocation Icebreakers, Session Norms "Seeing" each other into the learning space.
Asking self-awakening/orienting questions	Introduce the topic by explaining why we need to learn about racial justice. Explain that this workshop will focus on the following objectives: By the end of this lessons, participants will: • Describe types of racism. (You may use the resource at the end of this chapter.) • Articulate the powerful, yet insidious, impact of racism on people and society. • Formulate a strategy for identifying social, economic, and cultural factors that impact on race in your community. Use the table on "Intersection of Perspective Transformation and Action Research" to develop a list of questions that need to be explored in depth.
Reflecting theologically	Complete the exercise "Blindness in the Body of Christ"
Enacting the next most faithful step.	• Based on the insights from this lesson, create a long-range plan for addressing racial injustice in your community. • Explain how you would use videos, computers, and the Internet to reinforce your plan.

WORKSHOP EXERCISES

8:30 a.m. – 9:00 a.m.	Invocation/Welcome Introductions/Community Building Creating a Hospitable Environment
9:00 a.m. – 12:00 noon	**Workshop Session 1** **Activity 1 – Curriculum** **Development** **Activity 2 – Case Analysis**
12:30 p.m. – 1:00 p.m.	Lunch
2:00 p.m. – 5:00 p.m.	**Workshop Session 2** **Activity 1 – Blindness in the Body** **of Christ** **Activity 2 – Types of Racism**
5:30 p.m. – 6:00 p.m.	Workshop Evaluation Closing Worship, Benediction, Dismissal

Learning Activity – Curriculum Development
1. How the views of the curriculum presented in this chapter be applied in religious organizations?
2. Do your personal views about the curriculum differ from those described above?
3. Describe the typical learning experience in your setting. How does it differ from the ideas in this chapter?

Case Analysis of Teaching and Learning
Jeff, a teacher in the adult Bible study program, knew only one way to teach. He wished he could install a zipper on the minds of the learners, unzip the seal, pour in the facts, and zip-lock the contraption to seal in the knowledge. Martha, the Director of Christian Education, cringed every time she heard him say this. She disagreed adamantly with this approach to teaching. In her opinion, people – especially adults – had to have a context for learning. They had to be able to connect new information to

their personal experiences. She believed that every adult learner brought to the learning situation a unique set of insights and examples and emotions.

All of these factors had to be taken into consideration in helping learners make a connection with the new information they received daily. Not only that, but they also had to be able to see the relevance between the biblical text and their experiences in everyday life. The real world was complex and couldn't be divided into neat dichotomies of black/white or good/bad. Everything had to be considered in context. One of Martha's mottos was, "If people can't learn in the way we teach, we have to teach in the way they learn." She would have to have a long conversation with Jeff before the next adult Bible study course began.

Case Study Analysis Guidelines

1. What are the presenting problems as they relate to curriculum, teaching, and learning?
2. Using relevant details from the case, identify the deeper issues if any. Evaluate the seriousness of the issues.
3. Reflect theologically on the issue(s) you identified?
4. Identify two or more alternative solutions based on your analysis and theological reflection. Describe a plan to implement your solution.

Case Analysis: "The Leather Tanning Factory"

Frank went to work every day at the Northrup Leather Tanning Company in Waukegan, which was a small town on Lake Michigan. In the early days, the town had attracted a wave of Eastern Europeans, Finns, and Swedes. Later, during the 1920s, the next round of manufacturing expansion, Waukegan's population went up about 75%, drawing upon African Americans and Southern whites. The tannery had recruited Southern blacks to work in its Waukegan plant during WW I, but had to build housing for these new employees because whites would not rent to them. The tannery was one of the oldest industries in Waukegan. By 1955, there were around 19,000 manufacturing jobs in the Waukegan-North Chicago economic complex.

Although Frank started out as a laborer at the plant, he dreamed of ascending the ranks to a position in management one day. He had a brilliant mind and was always trying to figure out a better way to do things. The company required its employees to pass an exam to obtain a promotion. Frank scored high on these tests of general knowledge, but because the company kept changing the cutoff, they failed him each time. Each time he got close to making the mark, the company shifted the line of demarcation, relegating Frank to a permanent position at the bottom of the ladder.

Even so, Frank took pride in his work. The leather-tanning business captivated him. Tanning entailed the process of treating skins and hides of animals to produce leather. Manufacturing a high-quality finished product involved many stages and employed a range of chemicals that were often dangerous to the environment if not disposed of properly. Another troublesome aspect tanning involved the use of large quantities of water, which needed to be disposed of safely because of the toxic residue it contained.

One of those chemicals, chromium sulfate, contributed to the quality of the end-product, making it more flexible, soft, and thin. Unabsorbed chromium produced a sludge that caused environmental problems and was toxic to organisms. One way to solve the problem was to recover and reuse waste chromium. As a waste management intervention, Frank was working on creating a process that used naturally occurring microbes to mitigate excessive contamination and reduce the metal concentrations in aqueous solutions.

Frank immersed himself in his work, spending many hours in his workshop, often bouncing ideas off of Hannah because she was a good listener. And she loved to see him work. Hannah noticed that Frank had a fascination for yellow note pads and mechanical pencils, which he used to write out formulas using notations that she did not understand. Every once in a while, she asked questions that made him think more deeply about what he was doing.

Frank figured that if he couldn't pass the company's screening tests, he would be able to get his foot on the ladder by sharing his invention with the company. One day, Frank came home depressed and angry. He had finally presented his ideas to management. He figured they could buy his idea from him, and if that failed, he could apply for a patent on his own. Management rejected his idea. They were taken aback because a black man had presumed to approach them as an equal. They had laughed in his face, called him uppity, and told him to stay in his place or there would be consequences.

After that, Frank was determined to get revenge. He knew that the company had been dumping chromium wastewater into Lake Michigan. But he had no proof. One night when he and his family were at the beach in Waukegan Harbor, he noticed a truck with a company logo drive up to the edge of the pier, remove the chain from the back of the pick-up bed, and unload several 55-gallon barrels, which two men dumped into the lake. Frank tried to figure out a way he could gather proof of this illegal activity. So, he planned on returning to the scene with his Polaroid camera to capture the whole thing on film. Although he continued to go to the lakefront at night, the truck never reappeared. That is, until one Friday night. They came back. One of the truck drivers looked over and saw him sitting on the rocks near the pier with his camera. They recognized him from the plant. The next day they told the boss about it. The boss confronted Frank. They got into an altercation, and the boss threatened to fire Frank if he didn't back down.

A week later there was a mysterious fire at the leather tanning plant. Is severely burned one of the wings of the plant, and caused extensive damage to the pickling section where they cowhides were chemically conditioned for the tanning phase. The company suspected that Frank had something to do with it and surveilled his every move for weeks.

Case Study Analysis Guidelines

1. What are the presenting problems as they relate to teaching about racial justice?
2. Using relevant details from the case, identify the deeper issues if any. Evaluate the seriousness of the issues.
3. Reflect theologically on the issue(s) you identified?
4. Identify two or more alternative solutions based on your analysis and theological reflection. Describe a plan to implement your solution.

Teaching about Racial Justice

Assume that you are responsible for creating a set of lessons to teach about various types of racial justice. Using the resources provided at the end of this chapter, Bloom's taxonomy of educational objectives, Madeline Hunter's guidelines, develop a set of lesson plans. Feel free to use resources in the Appendix on Teaching About Racial Justice.

Case Analysis: Blindness in the Body of Christ

The exercise is based on scripture – the healing of the blind man at Bethsaida. As you read the scripture, think about what you have experienced or observed about systemic racism and the role of the community church. Additional definitions and resources are provided at the end of this chapter.

Mark 8:22-26 (NRSV) - [22] They came to Bethsaida. Some people brought a blind man to him and begged him to touch him. [23] He took the blind man by the hand and led him out of the village; and when he had put saliva on his eyes and laid his hands on him, he asked him, "Can you see anything?" [24] And the man looked up and said, "I can see people, but they look like trees, walking." [25] Then Jesus laid his hands on his eyes again, and he looked intently and his sight was restored, and he saw everything. [26] Then he sent him away to his home, saying, "Do not even go into the village."

Questions for Discussion and Reflection

1. In what ways does racism render us blind in the body of Christ. Cite examples of the following types of blindness we encounter in our human relations.
    a. Social Blindness
    b. Situational Blindness
    c. Spiritual Blindness
2. Discuss how and why others might have a worldview that is different from your own?

Discussion: Types of Racism

The definitions below are from the Alberta Civil Liberties Research Centre.[46] You may find this resource helpful as you plan lessons and facilitate discussions about racial injustice. Discuss each type of racism and share examples you have observed.

Systemic Racism includes the policies and practices entrenched in established organizations, which result in the exclusion or promotion of designated groups. It differs from overt discrimination in that no individual intent is necessary.

Institutional racism occurs within organizations and systems of power. This refers to the unfair policies and discriminatory practices of particular organizations (schools, workplaces, etc.) that routinely produce racially inequitable outcomes for people of color and advantages for white people. Individuals within organizations take on the power of the organization when they reinforce racial inequities. Some forms of this racism may include Jim Crow Laws in the US or the exclusion of African-American golfers from elite, private golf courses in the US, for example. Benefits are structured to privilege powerful groups at the expense of others.

Structural racism is a racial bias among organizations and across society. This involves the cumulative and compounding effects of an array of societal factors, including the history, culture, ideology, and interactions of organizations and policies that systematically privilege white people and disadvantage people of color. It refers to how the joint operation of organizations (i.e., inter-institutional arrangements and interactions) produce racialized outcomes, even in the absence of racist intent. Because these effects are reinforced across multiple organizations, the root causes of structural racism are difficult to isolate. Structural racism is cumulative, pervasive, and durable.

Internalized racism lies within individuals. This type of racism comprises one's private beliefs and biases about race and racism, influenced by one's culture. This can take many different forms including prejudice towards others of a different race; internalized oppression—the negative beliefs about oneself by people of color; or internalized privilege—beliefs about superiority or entitlement by white people.

Interpersonal racism occurs between individuals. This is the bias that occurs when individuals interact with others and their personal racial beliefs affect their public interactions. It is the holding of negative attitudes towards a different race or culture.

Individual racism refers to an individual's racist assumptions, beliefs, or behaviors. It is connected to/learned from broader socio-economic histories and processes and is supported and reinforced by systemic racism. Because we live in such a culture of individualism (and with the privilege of freedom of speech), some people argue that their statements/ideas are not racist because they are just "personal opinion." Here, it is important to point out how individualism functions to erase hierarchies of power, and to connect unrecognized personal ideologies to larger racial or systemic ones. (ACLC http://www.aclrc.com/glossary)

"Recognizing microaggressions." Microaggressions are the intentional or unintentional verbal, nonverbal, and environmental slights, snubs, or insults that communicate negative messages to target persons based solely upon their group membership. The table in this link describes common forms and themes associated with microaggressions. Available at: https://www.nhcucc.org/uploads/documents/conference-ministries/justice-witness-ministry/Racial%20Justice/RJMG%20-%20Microaggressions%20Examples.pdf

SUGGESTED RESOURCES

Selected Resources for Teaching about Racial Justice

Alberta Civil Liberties Centre. *CARED glossary*. Retrieved from
     http://www.aclrc.com/glossary

Annie Casey Foundation. *Equity vs. equality and other racial justice
     definitions*. Retrieved from
     https://www.aecf.org/blog/racial-justice-
     definitions/?gclid=CjwKCAjwlbr8BRA0EiwAnt4MTpo1
     AtcRxyOtU5D63kzEOLlwimx9ZtFoH-
     wkGxLFrsUUyHtbKPcENBoCHHMQAvD_BwE

Anti-Defamation League. *Personal self-assessment of anti-bias
     behavior*. Retrieved from
     https://www.adl.org/sites/default/files/documents/asset
     s/pdf/education-outreach/Personal-Self-Assessment-of-
     Anti-Bias-Behavior.pdf

Anti-Defamation League. *Race talk: engaging young people in
     conversations about race and racism*. Retrieved from
     https://www.adl.org/education/resources/tools-and-
     strategies/race-talk-engaging-young-people-in-
     conversations-about

Christian Church in Illinois and Wisconsin (CCIW) (Disciples
     of Christ). *God's shalom. justice and wholeness in today's world
     transforming the narrative for healing and wholeness, with Rev.
     David Anderson Hooker*. Retrieved from
     https://www.youtube.com/watch?v=DrPZZcRI-
     KQ&feature=youtu.be

National Council of Churches. *Anti-racism resources*. Retrieved
     from https://nationalcouncilofchurches.us/anti-racism-
     resources/

Slow North. *Journal prompts to help you engage self-reflection & check
     your white privilege*. Retrieved from

https://www.slownorth.com/blogs/journal/journal-prompts-to-help-you-engage-self-reflection-check-your-white-privilege

Stevenson, Bryan. *Changing America's racial narrative.* https://www.youtube.com/watch?v=jzPUmQfo3B8

UCC. White privilege – Let's talk. Retrieved from http://privilege.uccpages.org/

United Methodist Church. North Carolina Conference. *9 things your church can do to fight racism - media center - NC conference.* Retrieved from https://nccumc.org/mediacenter/9-things-your-church-can-do-to-fight-racism/

"Sacred Conversation on Race Resource Guide." The Sacred Conversation on Race can take many forms and there are many points of entry. Your Sacred Conversation will also evolve and change over time. It is our hope that you view this Sacred Conversation as a journey over time, and that your initial round of conversations prove to be only the first leg of that journey. Available at: http://d3n8a8pro7vhmx.cloudfront.net/unitedchurchofchrist/legacy_url/393/Sacred-Conversation-on-Race-Resource-Guide-NEW-small.pdf?1418423758

PART III: LEADERSHIP COMPETENCIES

Chapter 7: Communicating Effectively

CHAPTER PREVIEW

Readings and exercises in this chapter will help you:

- Facilitate effective communication within and on behalf of the church.
- Engage productively in public discourse.
- Communicate respectfully and effectively in diverse settings.

COMMUNICATION THEORY

Communication is complex and entails awareness of many variables that might interfere with meaning. Sometimes the lack of clear communication in the ministerial setting may lead to misunderstanding, mistakes in carrying out instructions, defiance of authority, and broken relationships, among other problems. Failure to communicate effectively also has implications for violations of the ministerial code of ethics (see Chapter 9 for more details).

The communication process involves complex steps. In the first step, a person (sender) wishes to convey a message. The sender is responsible for tapping into their long and short-term memory to retrieve the images, symbols, and concepts to be conveyed. These elements of the message are colored by the sender's past experiences and emotions. Keeping the audience (receiver) in mind, the sender will construct the message. This step is known as *ideating*. In the next step, the sender will encode the message. That is, the sender will select the words and symbols to be used to get the point across. This step is known as *encoding*. After the message is encoded, it must be *transmitted* through a channel. You will probably remember the words of McLuhan who said the "medium is the message." In many respects this notion is still valid today.

After the message is sent, the receiver takes over. At the *receiving* end, the message must be heard or seen, or experienced in some way. The receiver then will engage in *decoding* or deciphering the message. This deciphering process is governed by all that the receiver brings to the settings – their prior experiences or emotions. The final step in the communication process involves the receiver acting on the message. If the communication process has been effective, the message that was sent will be the message that was received.

EFFECTIVE COMMUNICATION

Ministerial leaders must have a keen understanding of the communication mechanisms in their settings so they will be able to facilitate a meeting of the minds with others in the organization. In any given setting, the ability to accomplish organizational goals depends on how well members communicate with each other and on how well the ministerial leader communicates with members. As communication mechanisms become more effective, the likelihood increases that the organization will be able to move toward its vision with a limited number of encumbrances.

Nonverbal Communication

Non-verbal mis-cues further complicate communication. Take a few minutes to consider how the following nonverbal cues may affect the message:

Personal appearance, possessions, demeanor
Kinesis (body movements and position)
- facial expression
- use of hands, arms, legs, and posture
- clothing

Paralanguage (voice qualities)
- voice quality, volume, speed, rate, pitch
- non-fluences (uh, ah, um)
- laughing, yawning, etc.

Proxemics (space and proximity)
- Intimate zone (0-2 feet)
- Personal zone (two-four feet)
- Social zone (four to twelve feet)
- Public zone (beyond twelve feet) strangers
- Physical space (appearance of space, comfort in invading space)

Chronemics (determinations and definitions of time)
- being late
- being on time

The direction of organizational communication
- Downward Communication
- Upward Communication
- Horizontal Communication - same hierarchical level
- Diagonal Communication
- The Grapevine

Barriers to Good Communication

The following is a listing of factors that act as additional barriers to effective communication. As you read each one, consider how they might have an impact on communication in your setting.

Frames of Reference - Members can interpret the same information differently depending on their level of learning, culture, and experience. Neither person's view is right nor wrong; those communicating just view the information differently.

Filtering - Transmittal of partial information to a sender. This is caused by differences in learning, culture, and experiences and results in distortions of information.

Structure - Communication efficiency decreases when an organization is hierarchical. This occurs because of changes, modifications, "filling in the blanks," and reinterpretations.

Information Overload - Technology increases the amount of information available. Members tend to engage in selective processing. As a result, they end up omitting, making errors, filtering, approximating, and avoiding information.

Semantics – Words have different meanings to different members. To communicate effectively common symbols must be used.

Status Differences – With higher status, there is less effective communication reception.

Subjectiveness of Communication

Frequently, the words and phrases we use serve to complicate understanding and therefore impede, rather than facilitate, communication. Among the factors that can make communication more complex are those that are culturally determined. The complex process of communication requires many steps involving the interpretation of images, symbols, and concepts on the part of both the sender and receiver.[47] Therefore, cultural diversity must be considered for effective communication.[48]

Social scientist Lisa Delpit has written extensively about diversity issues in communication. She contends that cross-cultural understanding becomes highly complicated when members are called on to communicate across social, racial, and cultural lines. She believes that successfully communicating in such situations requires listening that engages not only the eyes and the ears but also the heart and the mind. She says this is so because we tend to "see" things, not through our eyes or "hear" things through our ears. Rather, we tend to filter information through our beliefs. She says that to communicate effectively with groups different from our own, we have to put our beliefs on hold temporarily and be able to look honestly at other members. What we see may not be flattering, but often examining these views may be the only way to initiate a dialogue among members from differing cultures.

Delpit makes us aware that we all see behaviors, information, and situations through our cultural lenses. She is careful to note that these lenses operate on an involuntary basis – often below the level of conscious awareness. This makes it difficult sometimes to interpret the behavior of others because our lenses are making it appear that our view is "simply the way it is."

Reflecting on your own experiences, analyzing your own culture, examining and comparing different perspectives, Delpit contends, are the actions you have to take to interpret across cultures. She believes that a fundamental goal of reform-minded leaders should be to see the world as others see it. She says that we must maintain the perspective that members are experts in their own lives. While members may not be acutely aware of all aspects of the outside world, they are most certainly the only authentic experts on their own experiences. She also notes that members are typically rational beings, and therefore act rationally. Although we may not understand their rationales, we have a responsibility to try to apprehend them. She concludes that we must allow ourselves to be vulnerable enough to permit the realities of others to enter into our consciousness. Then, and only then, is effective cross-cultural communication possible. Awareness of barriers to effective communication may help alleviate this problem.

Improving Cross-cultural Communication

Improving cross-cultural competence in communication may involve participation in activities that adhere to a common communication code based on sensitivity, awareness, and ability. Intercultural awareness results in enhancing not only cultural sensitivity but also self-awareness. Your intercultural competence might be improved through cross-cultural knowledge training that raises awareness about the differences in values beliefs, perceptions, interpretations.[49] Ministerial leaders should strive to move toward establishing a universally accepted culture in which everyone understands the other person's values and beliefs and respects them. Leaders should further commit to building an organizational climate without conflicts and differences of opinion. Doing so will contribute to overcoming cross-cultural barriers.

Active (Empathetic) Listening

Communication involves not only speaking but also listening. Madelyn Burley-Allen offers these guidelines for empathic listening.[50] Perhaps one of the most important guidelines is to be attentive. Engage in the conversation by showing interest, being alert and not distracted, and creating a positive atmosphere through nonverbal behavior.

Being a sounding board is another guideline. That means allowing your conversation partner to bounce ideas and feelings off you while assuming a nonjudgmental, non-critical manner. It is acceptable to act like a mirror when the speaker is talking. That means to reflect what you think the speaker is saying or feeling. However, be careful not to "grill" the speaker by asking a lot of clarifying questions. Sometimes the goal is to generate creativity. Don't discount the speaker's feelings by using stock phrases like "It's not that bad," or "You'll feel better tomorrow." Also, do not let the speaker "hook" you. This can happen if you get angry or upset, allow yourself to get involved in an argument, or pass judgment on the other person.

Indicate you are listening by providing brief, noncommittal acknowledgments, e.g., "Uh-huh," "I see." Give nonverbal acknowledgments, e.g., head nodding, facial expressions matching the speaker, open and relaxed body expression, eye contact. Invite the speaker to say more, e.g., "Tell me about it," "I'd like to hear about that."

Burley-Allen has also indicated that you should follow good listening "ground rules," such as the ones bulleted below:

- Don't interrupt.
- Don't change the subject or move in a new direction.
- Don't rehearse in your head.
- Don't interrogate.
- Don't teach.
- Don't give advice.

Remember, the ability to listen with empathy may be the most important attribute of ministerial leaders who succeed in gaining the trust and cooperation of parties to intractable conflicts and other disputes with high emotional content. Providing an opportunity for members to talk through their problems may clarify their thinking as well as provide a necessary emotional release.

Communication Responding Formats

Open-ended question	Allow wide range for response
Closed-ended question	Limit range of response
Confirmatory paraphrase	Clarify real underlying meaning
Leading paraphrase	Influence-reexamination of thinking (clear up incongruity)

- Share an account of when the formats worked or did not work to enhance your communication.
- In pairs or groups identify when each of the formats could be used appropriately in your setting (i.e., meeting, memo, phone call, other).

WRITING CLEARLY

As you already know, writing is another important form of communication. You should start by considering the purposes of your writing and carefully plan how you will achieve that purpose. Included in this section, you will find guidelines to help you reach your readers successfully.

Use personal pronouns such as "you" and "I," as if you were speaking directly to the reader. Use illustrations (figures, tables), and examples. "A picture is worth a thousand words." Use short sentences and paragraphs. Use active verbs. Active words have an impact. Use only necessary words. Use a structure that resembles an outline, including ample headings and subheadings. Use chunking (i.e., lists of key points, accented by numbers or bullets). Use techniques of emphasis (e.g., boldface, italics) to accent important ideas.

You should also consider how your intended audience will receive what you have written. This depends on how well you have chosen your words. Are you getting your point across effectively?

Limit your use of jargon—language specific to your trade, profession, or group. An essay for a layperson should have very little jargon if any; however, an essay for a specialist may incorporate technical terms. If in doubt, err on the side of less jargon. It will be difficult to retain your readers' interest if they must constantly refer to a dictionary.

Choose an appropriate level of formality. Generally, you can be informal with personal correspondence and personal narratives; however, you must be formal with business correspondence and most academic essays (research papers, etc.). Consider your position to the reader. If the recipient or reader has the authority to approve/deny a proposal request, to provide performance reviews, etc., always err on the side of formality.

Avoid sexist language. These days, it isn't acceptable to use the masculine as a stand-in for all members or *his* as a default when writing in the singular. You may use *his or her or them*, but often your writing will flow better if you can rework the sentence to avoid the issue entirely or if you can convert your nouns and pronouns to the plural form.

Avoid euphemisms – more pleasant words substituted for harsh realities – if possible. Certainly, some euphemisms are both commonplace and acceptable – for example, *passed away* is a common euphemism for *dying*. However, most euphemisms merely serve to obscure meaning and render your document wordy (*pre-owned automobile for a used car*, for example).

Avoid slang. Not only do you risk confusing an audience unfamiliar with these terms, but your work, 10 years from now, may appear dated. When you select words, consider their connotations – that is, their implied meanings. This is especially true in communicating across cultures.

Use specific nouns and active verbs. For example, only use the word *thing* when you have no other alternative. This word is dull and vague. Further, whenever possible, avoid *being* verbs such as *is*, *am*, and *were*. Sometimes this verb is necessary – for instance, in definitions – but, in many cases, an alternate choice will make your sentence more lively and concise.

Avoid clichés and use figures of speech sparingly. Clichés are overused figures of speech, such as similes and metaphors that have lost their impact—for example, white as a ghost. Thus, your best bet is to describe the situation, person, etc., in your own words. Original figures of speech, however, can be effective, but use them in moderation.

Use metaphors sparingly. Metaphors engage your readers because they are uncommon. However, too many metaphors strung together can diminish their impact and even prove confusing if you do not develop a single comparison.

MULTIMEDIA PRESENTATIONS

Presentation Behavior

We live in an age where the use of multimedia is commonplace. PowerPoint presentations, in particular, should be viewed as a potent tool if used effectively. This section provides some suggestions for improving your multimedia presentations. One problem with computer-generated PowerPoint slides is that the speaker and the audience tend to focus on the slide. You should talk to the audience, not the screen. Minimize looking at the slide and spend time looking at the audience. This will make it easier to make eye contact with them.

Consider reducing your PowerPoint slides to bulleted items. A rule of thumb is to include no more than twenty-four words per slide. Use a large enough font size for the slide to be viewed at a distance of at least twenty feet. Keep the slide in view long enough for the audience to grasp its meaning. Depending on the setting, you might want to provide your audience with your PowerPoint slides. You may do this electronically. The other alternative is to provide a hard copy the audience may use as a "takeaway" from the meeting.

Organizing Your Presentation

Many leaders use PowerPoint presentations (or similar software) to keep them organized during an oral presentation. If you cannot memorize the content of your presentation, practice reading it with as much enthusiasm – variation in pitch, tone, and modulation of your voice, as well as periodic eye contact with your audience – as possible. The trick to reading a talk (or presentation) is to appear not to be reading it.

During the question portion of your presentation, maintain eye contact with the questioner while periodically scanning the entire audience. In a large meeting, you might repeat the question for all to hear using a microphone.

Arranging your slides will also have an impact on how well it is received by your audience. Consider the following guidelines:

- Begin with a title slide (include the title of your project, your name, affiliation, and date)
- Provide a slide that outlines your presentation
- Present a concise overview of your topic
- Include 1-2 slides for each major point
- Use figures and diagrams liberally
- Avoid cluttering your slides with dense details
- Use at least an 18-point font
- Conclude with no more than two slides outlining a summary of your conclusions and recommendations

WORKSHOP EXERCISES

8:30 a.m. – 9:00 a.m.	Invocation/Welcome Introductions/Community Building Creating a Hospitable Environment
9:00 a.m. – 12:00 noon	**Workshop Session 1** **Activity 1 – Overcoming Barriers** **Activity 2 – Enhancing** **Communication**
12:30 p.m. – 1:00 p.m.	Lunch
2:00 p.m. – 5:00 p.m.	**Workshop Session 2** **Activity 1 – Cross Cultural Issues** **Activity 2 – Skills Worksheet**
5:30 p.m. – 6:00 p.m.	Workshop Evaluation Closing Worship, Benediction, Dismissal

Ways to Overcome Communication Barriers

Repetition	Same message, multiple channels, face-to-face meetings.
Empathy	Attempting to share a frame of reference.
Understanding	Attempt to use simple, understandable language.
Feedback	Verbal and visual cues that the message was understood, one-on-one conversations.
Listening:	Attempting to really "hear" what the other person is saying.

- Take a few minutes to think about each of the barriers listed. Recall a time when one or more of the barriers interfered with your effectively communicating a message.

- Overcoming the communication barriers involves considering the impact of what you say before you speak. With a groupmate, generate a list of ways you may use one or more of the following mechanisms to positively impact how your message is received.

Learning Activity: Cross-Cultural Concerns

- Assess the effectiveness of your conversations with people from other cultures or racial groups. What makes them effective? Ineffective?
- Identify ways you could improve your cross-cultural conversations?

Ways to Enhance Communication

Stop talking.	Ask for more information.	Problem-solve together.
Give your full attention.	Rephrase the questions or statements.	Show empathy.
Validate the other person's feelings.	Put talker at ease.	Stay silent until the other person is finished talking.
Withhold judgment.	Remove distractions.	Use "yes … and" statements.
Empathize with the talker.	Be patient.	Hold your temper.
Go easy on argument and criticism.		

- Review the ways to enhance communication listed in the table above.

- In pairs or groups, describe how you might use some of these enhancers to improve communication in your organizational setting.

Personal Experience: Think about your unique setting. Briefly describe an experience you had involving miscommunication. What went wrong? What was challenging? How did you resolve the issue(s)?

Case Study Analysis: "Sharon Fitzgerald"

Carrie Mae is one of your parishioners. She works at the local school and has recently returned from disciplinary meeting. She is very upset and asks for your input. Read the case below. Then answer the case analysis questions.

***

When Michael returned from his three-day suspension, all parties involved had to attend an obligatory re-entry conference. Michael's mother, Charlene, asked Carrie Mae to accompany her to Michael's meeting. Francine Parkinson leafed through a stack of papers as she waited for everyone to arrive.

The conference was scheduled to begin at 4 p.m., but Sharon Fitzgerald was late. She walked into the meeting at 4:25 without an apology or explanation.

After preliminary remarks and everyone was settled, Charlene asked Sharon to provide a precise definition for assault, class disruption and "defiance of authority." Sharon went into colorful detail about what happened the day of the suspension. When Sharon had finished relating her version of the story, Charlene exploded.

"Don't get me wrong. I know my son is not an angel, but I don't think for one minute that my son meant to assault you. I understand that everyone was tossing around paper wads. As to class disruption, it sounds like he was stating his opinion in a reasonable way. I don't get the defiance-of-authority part. Exactly how was Michael defying your so-called authority?"

Charlene protested loudly. "It sounds like brilliant reasoning to me!"

"Believe me. Michael was defiant and persistent and loud. Louder than most of them. Even after I asked him to be quiet several times, he kept on arguing with me. Because of his incessant arguing, other students started to misbehave. I had no alternative but to write him up."

"Excuse me? He didn't do anything wrong." Charlene expressed her indignation.

Sharon immediately bristled.

"I don't have to explain myself to you or anyone," Sharon said. "I am the math teacher, and you will respect my rights to manage my classroom."

"Look here, lady. I'm not trying to disrespect you. I just want to find out why my child keeps getting referrals in your class," Charlene responded.

"That's simple. Michael flatly refuses to work cooperatively with the other students. His homework is never in the proper format. He always challenges me on every count. Whenever I introduce a new concept, he always comes up with these far-fetched notions and hangs onto them like a bulldog. When I try to correct him, he flies off the handle. Besides that, he's totally radical, he's threatening, and he's rude."

"Then maybe you ought to write me up, Mrs. Fitzgerald, because that's how I raised my son. But the fact remains. You still haven't answered my question. How are the things you just described classified as defying authority? Please, please help me understand."

Charlene flailed her arms out of frustration. As she continued to protest, a belligerent edge crept into Charlene's voice. To emphasize her point, she, stood up and started to pace the length of the room. Sharon Fitzgerald shifted uncomfortably in her chair. Carrie Mae just looked at Charlene.

"I don't have to tolerate this," Sharon Fitzgerald finally screeched wildly. "I can see where Michael gets his obnoxious behavior. It's just the kind of thing I would expect from you people."

The room grew silent.

"You people?" Charlene responded.

"Mrs. Parkinson, aren't you going to say anything?" Sharon shouted.

Francine said nothing. Sharon was saying enough for the both of them.

"I don't have to stand for this kind of treatment from anyone. In fact, I'm going to report all of you to the superintendent and the union," Sharon shouted.

Then Sharon Fitzgerald stormed out of the room.

Case Study Analysis Guidelines

1. What are the presenting problems as they relate to cross-cultural communication?
2. Using relevant details from the case, identify the deeper issues, if any. Evaluate the seriousness of the issues.
3. Reflect theologically on the issue(s) you identified?
4. Identify two or more alternative solutions based on your analysis and theological reflection. Describe a plan to implement your solution.

SUGGESTED RESOURCES

Learning Activity: Skills Worksheet
Review and discuss the **"Effective, Cross-Cultural Communication Skills Worksheet."** Available at:
https://hclsig.thinkculturalhealth.hhs.gov/ProviderContent/PDFs/EffectiveCrossCulturalComm.pdf

"Intercultural Training Exercise Pack," Available at:
https://www.ambitia.eu/wp-content/uploads/2019/02/2%20Intercultural%20Trainig%20Exercise%20Pack.pdf

"Interactive Methods for Teaching about Cultural Differences," (Wake Forest University). Available at: https://prod.wp.cdn.aws.wfu.edu/sites/18/2016/03/Bennett. Janet_.2016.pdf

"Effective Cross-Cultural Communication Skills Worksheet," Available at: https://hclsig.thinkculturalhealth.hhs.gov/ProviderContent/P DFs/EffectiveCrossCulturalComm.pdf

Chapter 8: Leading the Organization

CHAPTER PREVIEW

Readings and exercises in this chapter will help you:

- Recognize the role of effective leadership.
- Identify the role of leadership in impacting systemic change.
- Describe the relationship between leadership and personality.
- Exercise conflict transformation through leadership.

THE VIEW FROM THE TOP

Effective leadership is essential for success in organizational settings, including ministerial settings. The term *leadership* means many things to different people. Unfortunately, almost everyone who studies or writes about leadership defines the construct differently. For example, Bennis and Nanus noted that more than 350 definitions of leadership are recorded in the literature.[51] Various theories attempt to explain what leaders do, how they behave, and the attributes they possess. One common definition is this: Leadership is the art of motivating a group of people to act toward achieving a common goal.

Work-role Definitions

Many people lump leadership together with administration, management, and supervision, even though subtle differences exist among these work roles. These work roles can be used in balanced integration to stimulate performance and address the needs of the organization.

Work Roles

Administrator	Leader
Administrators provide support to either an individual or team to facilitate the smooth operation of an organization.	Leaders set direction, build an inspiring vision, establish a culture and create new directions and outcomes.
Specific responsibilities may include:	**Specific responsibilities may include:**
• Planning, organizing, and controlling • Efficient deployment of people, resources and information • Ensuring that the team meets its goals, and they have all the resources they need to do so • Managing data and reports • Keeping records up to date • Helping maintain the budget plan • Handling technical issues in their area of expertise	• Creating a vision and providing strategic direction of an organization • Inspiring people and creating visions and ideas • Establishing a culture and creating conditions that facilitate movement toward a common goal • Inspiring members of the organization to achieve their potential • Developing strategies for continuous improvement • Communicating with internal and external stakeholders to share the vision

Work Roles (continued)

Supervisor	Manager
Supervisors communicate organizational needs, oversee employees' performance, and plan workloads, allocate tasks and monitor progress against targets	Managers plan, coordinate, and clarify objectives. They oversee programs, delegate tasks, and provide feedback on task performance.
Specific responsibilities may include: • Overseeing the work and performance of employees • Ensuring that the work is completed on time and monitoring the accuracy of work • Compiling staff rosters, dealing with leave requests and arranging to cover when necessary • Recruiting, training and helping staff reach their professional development goals • Devising work schedules and implementing deadlines • Assigning tasks and ensuring timely and accurate completion • Ensuring that professional standards are upheld • Conducting performance reviews	**Specific responsibilities may include:** • Making essential decisions that affect all areas of operation • Matching employees and the duties they must perform to ensure the completion of tasks • Allocating resources to accomplish specific goals • Setting performance goals and overseeing the success of a team • Identifying, interviewing and hiring employees • Communicating information to employees • Evaluating employee performance • Streamlining workflow, communication and performance • Developing work schedules and monitoring vacations, paid time off, and emergencies

Leadership and Culture

Mitchell and Tucker[52] observed that some organizations exist in community cultures where there is broad-ranged support based on a consensus about the purposes and processes of the organization. By contrast, in other organizations, typically those that are likely to encounter negative circumstances due to economic and social reasons, people are often challenged to change their goals while at the same time performing in traditional areas. Therefore, the work-roles may vary, depending on the cultural context and circumstances of the task to be performed.

The difference between these two cultural settings is much like the difference between frontier life and settled communities. In frontier cultures, life is rough, the danger is everywhere, and groups have to band together for mutual support and protection. Frontier leadership emphasizes culture building and problem-solving with a shared commitment to the emerging community. Settled cultures, on the other hand, are characterized by well-established norms and shared beliefs. These communities have stable practices and programs with tasks and relationships that are well specified.[53]

LCDSS Screening Scale

The concepts of leadership and culture have been studied separately for decades. As part of my dissertation research, I developed a model to show that the personal characteristics of organizational executives, their organizational environments, and the kinds of communities in which they work influence their leadership work-role, style, and emphasis. The *Leadership-Culture Dimensional Screening Scale (LCDSS)* was designed to measure the relationship between frontier and settlement cultures; transactional and transformational leadership styles; and the four work-roles (supervisor, administrator, manager, leader) formed by the intersection of the culture and leadership dimensions. The major premise was that organizational executives may employ all four work-role orientations to accomplish specific tasks, but the executive's dominant work-role orientation must match that of the culture. The concept was tested on school principals and showed that transactional leaders tended to exhibit preferences related to the work-roles of Managers and Supervisors, while transformational leaders exhibited characteristics of the Administrator and Leader work-roles. As a result of this research, I concluded that both the leadership characteristics and the community culture must be considered if organizational performance is to remain stable or improve.[54]

Organizational Complexity

Contributing to organizational complexity is the fact that churches are inherently part of larger structures, which change very slowly. Terrence E. Deal[55] believes that revolutionary changes in these organizations are rare because they occupy a special place in a community, and they serve as storehouses of our memories. He believes that transforming complex organizations must entail a fundamental renegotiation of "cherished myths and sacred rituals by multiple constituencies." The entire community must reweave or reshape the symbolic tapestry that gives meaning to the processes that take place in these institutions. He emphasizes that no plan to improve these organizational settings makes sense unless there is reasonable clarity about what the change involves and what constitutes "better."

Thomas Sergiovanni asserted that leadership must be responsive to what the cultural "centers" demand.[56] He said that centers safeguard the values, sentiments, and beliefs that provide the needed cement for uniting people in a common cause. Centers govern the religious organizational values and provide norms that guide behavior and give meaning to community life. Centers respond to questions like, What is this religious organization about? What is our image of congregants? How do we work together as members of a beloved community? Simply put, the leader must be able to exert a certain style of operating within the community so that the followers are responsive. You can conclude from the preceding discussion that both the leadership and the community must be taken into consideration if improved organizational performance is to occur. The leadership must be able to work within the context of the culture to affect outcomes in productive ways.

The church is no exception. According to Newport, "There is little doubt that outstanding church leadership can be a powerful factor in facilitating the degree to which parishioners feel closer to God, learn how to become better people, and get comfort in times of trouble and sorrow."[57] Outstanding ministerial leaders will be those who can manage the affairs of the church or ministry and have a warm and caring attitude toward their parishioners. Servant leadership provides a viable model.

Servant Leadership

Servant leader theory says that the most effective leaders are those who are willing to be servants first, leading from a desire to better serve others and not to attain more power. Robert Greenleaf asserted, "Servant leadership is a philosophy and set of practices that enrich the lives of individuals, builds better organizations, and ultimately creates a more just and caring world."[58] To that end, Greenleaf identified "12 Characteristics of Servant Leaders," which are summarized below for your convenience.

1. **Listening:** Any successful traditional leader will tell you that communication and decision-making are important factors in their ability to influence their constituents positively. Servant-leaders are no different. They, too, must convey a commitment to listening to others intently. Active listening helps the leader

"identify and clarify the will of a group." Therefore, servant-leaders listen receptively to what is said as well as to what is done by others. Greenleaf has reported that "listening also encompasses getting in touch with one's inner voice, and seeking to understand what is being communicated."

2. **Empathy:** Understanding and empathizing with others is another behavior that servant-leaders exhibit. They try to look for the special and unique characteristics of others. They make so-called spirit-to-spirit connections with those whom they serve. Having empathy also entails assuming "the good intentions of employees/partners and not rejecting them as people, even when forced to reject or call into question their behavior or performance."

3. **Healing:** Greenleaf noted: "One of the great strengths of servant-leadership is the potential for healing oneself and others." Healing is essential if growth and renewal, integration, and transformation are to take place. In *The Servant as Leader*, Greenleaf wrote, "There is something subtle communicated to those being served and led if implicit in the compact between the servant-leader and led is the understanding that the search for wholeness is something that they have."

4. **Awareness:** This characteristic pertains to self-awareness as well as awareness of the needs of others. Servant-leaders who are aware have a strong sensitivity for what is going on. They scan the environment to note the subtleties and nuances that occur. "They are always looking for cues from their opinions and decisions. They know what's going on and will rarely be fooled," according to Greenleaf. In doing so, servant leaders can respond more readily when action is required.

5. **Persuasion:** Servant-leaders cultivate skill in persuading others, rather than relying on positional authority or coercion in making decisions. Servant leaders convince others to comply with what is needed. Having the ability to persuade is "one of the clearest distinctions between the traditional authoritarian model and that of servant-leadership," according to Greenleaf.

Having the skill to persuade becomes important when it is necessary to build consensus within groups.

6. **Conceptualization:** Servant-leaders are people who "dream great dreams," according to Greenleaf. This involves looking at the organization and the issues that emerge and conceptualize fresh approaches to problem-solving. Greenleaf calls this thinking beyond the day-to-day realities. At the same time, servant-leaders have to be able to strike a delicate balance between conceptualization and day-to-day focus.

7. **Foresight:** Servant-leaders are visionary leaders who can "understand lessons from the past, the realities of the present, and the likely consequence of a decision in the future. It is deeply rooted in the intuitive mind," according to Greenleaf.

8. **Stewardship:** Servant-leaders with a strong sense of stewardship are those willing to prepare the organization to contribute to the greater good of society. Thus, they are responsible for "preparing it for its destiny," according to Greenleaf.

9. **Growth:** Servant leaders take responsibility for helping people grow. They believe that all members of the organization have something to offer beyond their tangible contributions. Servant-leaders, then, make concerted attempts to connect to the developmental needs of others and actively find ways to help them reach their true potential.

10. **Building Community:** Servant-leaders possess and convey a strong sense of "community spirit and work hard to foster it in an organization." Believing the organization should function as a community, they work hard to build cohesiveness from within. Greenleaf asserts, "Servant-leaders are aware that the shift from local communities to large organizations as the primary shaper of humanity has changed our perceptions and caused a sense of loss." Accordingly, servant-leaders try to find the means for building community among those who are part of the larger organization.

11. **Calling:** Servant-leaders have a natural desire to attend to others and are willing to sacrifice self-interest for the good of the organization. According to Greenleaf, "This notion of having a calling to serve is deeply rooted and values-based." Leaders who are also servants desire to make a difference among others in the organization and do their best to pursue opportunities that impact the lives of everyone in the community. They never act solely for their gain.

12. **Nurturing the Spirit:** Servant-leaders are people who nurture the spirits of those in the organization. They accomplish this by praising organizational members honestly and supporting them by recognizing their efforts. When the servant-leader must give criticism, the criticism is offered without harshness. Greenleaf observed that the servant-leader "reminds employees to reflect on the importance of both the struggles and successes in the organization and learn from both."

Leadership Styles

The term *leadership style* pertains to the leader's preferred methods for influencing subordinates and directing, planning, implementing, motivating, and generally ensuring that the organizational goals are accomplished. Servant Leadership is one of many leadership styles. Other styles may include autocratic, bureaucratic, authoritarian, delegative, democratic, participative, transactional, transformational, charismatic, coaching, and collaborative. Keeping up with all the definitions may be challenging; you can find detailed descriptions for these styles on various websites. For example, Indeed.com has defined ten common leadership styles on their website.[59] New styles emerge as research continues.

Leadership and Personality

Studies have examined leadership and personality type in relation to one another in recent years. One's leadership qualities and personality traits typically complement each other, although research results have been mixed.[60] Nevertheless, many investigations attempt to assess the personality types with the understanding that this information can be helpful in contributing to self-understanding. Two of these assessments are the Meyer's-Briggs Type Indicator and the Enneagram Type Indicator.

The Myers-Briggs Type Indicator (MBTI®) is an assessment tool used for self-awareness and improvement. Through a series of questions, the MBTI assessment helps you identify your natural preferences in four areas of personality:

- How do you direct and receive energy—by focusing on the outside world, interacting with people and taking action, or by focusing on your inner world and reflecting on ideas, memories, and experiences?
- How do you take in information—by focusing on what you perceive using your five senses or by seeing the big picture and looking for relationships and patterns?
- How do you decide and come to conclusions—by logically analyzing the situation or by considering what's important to the people involved?
- How do you approach the outside world—in a planned, orderly way or a more flexible, spontaneous way?

Your natural preferences in these four areas place you into one of 16 distinct MBTI personality types. "Understanding these types gives you objective insight that you can use to enhance your professional and personal relationships, as well as your direction, focus, and choices."[61]

The Enneagram Type Indicator is another tool that helps people to see themselves on a deeper level and provides insight into their relationships with other people. The Enneagram employs a very old typology that describes nine different characteristics. According to Richard Rohr, "Each of the nine types embraces a broad spectrum, which we can imagine as a continuous scale that runs between the extremes of 'immature' and 'mature'."[62]

In their book, *The Road Back to You*, Cron and Stabile provide a summary of these types:[63]

Type One – The Perfectionist
Type Two – The Helper
Type Three – The Performer
Type Four – The Romantic
Type Five – The Investigator
Type Six – The Loyalist
Type Seven – The Enthusiast
Type Eight – The Challenger
Type Nine – The Peacemaker

The authors state,

> *"The nine numbers on the Enneagram are divided into three triads —three in the Heart or Feeling Triad, three in the Head or Fear Triad, and three in the Gut or Anger triad. Each of the three numbers in each triad is driven in different ways by an emotion related to a part of the body known as a center of intelligence. Basically, your triad is another way of describing how you habitually take in, process and respond to life."[64]*

Practical Skills For Leadership

Ministry is my third career. Because of my prior training and experience in educational administration and my doctoral studies in the field of leadership, it has been easy to transpose my skill as an administrator, manager, supervisor, and leader to the ministerial setting. My gifts have not changed. Rather, I have learned to adapt them to my new circumstances. I've discovered that effective ministerial leaders are those who can assess the setting, discern a Godly vision, and articulate that vision in such a way that the constituents will follow, and the organization thrive. Today's ministerial learners will have to be versatile thinkers to manage the rapid changes and complexities they will face. If churches and other ministries are to be responsive to the different needs and talents of congregants, they must be organized to allow for variability rather than to assume uniformity. There is little room in today's society for leaders who cannot manage complexity, find and use resources, and continually learn new technologies, approaches, and occupations.

During your lifetime, you also may have developed leadership skills and dispositions you can use in a range of settings. Hopefully, you will discover that serving in the leadership role is a synergistic experience in which the whole is more than the sum of its parts. This chapter can help you discern your options.

WORKSHOP EXERCISES

8:30 a.m. – 9:00 a.m.	Invocation/Welcome Introductions/Community Building Creating a Hospitable Environment
9:00 a.m. – 12:00 noon	**Workshop Session 1** **Activity 1 – Ministerial Platform** **Activity 2 – Case Study**
12:30 p.m. – 1:00 p.m.	Lunch
2:00 p.m. – 5:00 p.m.	**Workshop Session 2** **Activity 1 – Challenges** **Activity 2 – Personal Experience**
5:30 p.m. – 6:00 p.m.	Workshop Evaluation Closing Worship, Benediction, Dismissal

Learning Activity: Developing a Ministerial Platform
Leadership effectiveness begins with knowing oneself. Often a ministerial leader may experience stresses that make the job seem to be a battleground. Too often routines become displaced by cultural conflict in the organization and the inevitable firefighting that occurs because of such conflict. The leader can reduce the potential for conflict and stress by taking an assessment of the various value systems that exist in the religious organizational setting. When the values of the leader and those of the organization are in harmony, things are likely to fall into place.

Behavioral research suggests that the most effective leaders are those who understand themselves, both their strengths and weaknesses. Self-understanding helps leaders develop strategies to meet the demands of their environment. Included here is a model designed to guide ministerial leaders as they assess their values, beliefs, and attitudes about ministry. The resulting platform is similar to those developed by political candidates and includes five major elements:

1. Aims of your ministry
2. Biblical basis for your ministry's activities
3. Desired achievements for your ministry
4. Leader's image of the ministry's members
5. Preferred kind of interacting with members

After reflecting on and clarifying your values and beliefs in these five areas, you will typically have an easier time articulating your visions of what should be occurring in the ministerial setting. Now, it's your turn to write your platform. Make sure you include and fully develop the five points listed above.

Learning Activity: Case Study – "Importance of the Interview"

Martha was looking forward to the upcoming interview. She considered the process to be a two-way yardstick. While the search committee was sizing her up, Martha would be able to make decisions regarding how well the church community measured up to her own personal belief structure. The interview would provide her with an opportunity to get a "feel" for the community and its culture. It was during this screening process that questions would be asked and answered regarding philosophies, styles, values, and practices. The process might also reveal certain tensions that existed as carry-overs from her predecessor and provide insight into why the previous pastor had left the job so abruptly. The process would further provide Martha an opportunity to engage in trust building with search committee members.

She'd been to enough interviews to know the drill. Sometimes a screening committee is in search of a mother figure to care for the "church family." In other cases, the committee may set its sights on finding a custodian who will carry out the rules and do what she is told. Still another committee may consider nothing short of a charismatic change agent. The interview process would give her a chance to assess the match between her talents and experience and the expectations of the prospective employer. Martha was excited about the possibilities and had thrown her hat into the ring in good faith.

Case Study Analysis Guidelines

1. What are the presenting problems as they relate to leadership in organizations?
2. Using relevant details from the case, identify the deeper issues if any. Evaluate the seriousness of the issues.
3. Reflect theologically on the issue(s) you identified?

4. Identify two or more alternative solutions based on your analysis and theological reflection. Describe a plan to implement your solution.

Learning Activity: Work Roles

Discuss the various definitions of leadership presented in this chapter? Describe examples of the four work roles in your ministry setting. Identify examples of exceptional leaders you have known. What characteristics or traits set them apart from others?

Learning Activity: Challenges

What special challenges exist for leaders in ministerial settings that do not exist in non-religious settings? What are some key situational and cultural factors that influence leadership in your setting?

Personal Experience:

Now think about your unique setting. Briefly describe an experience you had involving leadership. What was rewarding about the experience? What was challenging?

SUGGESTED RESOURCES

The Marks of Faithful and Effective Authorized Ministers is a tool for discernment and assessment, created especially for use by Members in Discernment, Committees on Ministry, and authorized ministers. The Marks emerged from conversations concerning definitions of "learnedness and leadership in authorized ministry" and to emphasize excellence in ministerial formation. The Marks provide a lens for reflecting upon your formation, gifts and growth both before authorization and throughout your ministry. Available at: http://uccfiles.com/pdf/THE-MARKS-OF-FAITHFUL-AND-EFFECTIVE-MINISTERS.pdf

"The Enneagram Type Indicator." Available
at https://tests.enneagraminstitute.com/orders/create

"The Strengths Finder." CliftonStrengths 34 is reported to
be one of the best ways for you to understand your talents and
maximize your potential. Available at:
https://store.gallup.com/p/en-us/10003/cliftonstrengths-34

"The Myer's Briggs Type Indicator." Available at:
https://www.mbtionline.com/

Additional Free Assessments
The following links may help you explore your gifts for
leadership independently. All are free of charge.

***"Behavioral Resource Group's* TARP Assessment."** This is
one of the 3 tools based on the work of the late Erich
Seligmann Fromm, a psychologist, psychoanalyst,
sociologist, and John G. Geier's original DISC model.
Available at: http://behavioralresourcegroup.com/free-disc-
personality-test/

"APEST." This spiritual gift assessment helps you in finding
your ministry style based on the fivefold ministry Paul lays out
in Ephesians 4—the five roles are outlined as Apostle,
Prophet, Evangelist, Shepherd and Teacher. Available at:
https://www.c3.nyc/apest-test

"True Colors Personality Assessment." True Colors is an
attempt to identify various personality styles and label them
with colors. This model of categorizing personality styles
draws heavily on the work of Isabel Briggs-Myers, Katherine
Briggs, and David Keirsey. Available at:
https://www.girlscoutsatl.org/content/dam/girlscouts-

girlscoutsatl/documents/GS-from-Home-True-Colors-
Quiz.pdf

Chapter 9: Administering Programs

CHAPTER PREVIEW

Readings and exercises in this chapter will help you:
- Explain the challenges of administration.
- Identify innovative patterns of staff development.
- Plan an effective meeting.
- Describe frameworks for collaborative problem-solving.
- Describe the purpose of a ministerial code of ethics.

FACILITATING GROWTH

Staff Development

As a ministerial leader, you may be placed in charge of staff or a group of parishioners to achieve a particular purpose. You may find it necessary to create opportunities for them to discuss important issues in meaningful and critical ways. That's where well-structured staff development programs come into play. Sometimes ministerial leaders pattern their staff-development offerings after what they have experienced.

Unfortunately, some of the staff-development programs you may have attended have not been well-structured. For example, too often, a so-called expert is brought in to engage in the latest rhetoric about religious reform. Participants, of course, are expected to absorb this information passively. Some of them sit near the back of the room and whisper to one another, while others are engaged with their electronic devices as the speaker drones on at the podium. Participants may look up every once in a while, at the typical PowerPoint. At some of these sessions, not only does the presenter visually project the PowerPoint show; but they also provide it in hard copy handouts, then read it to those sitting in the room.

Participants in these sessions might have concerns about the information being disseminated, yet they are not allowed to ask questions. Their only interaction with other participants may occur during contrived small-group breakouts that require participants to briefly discuss a set of questions they have been given and to designate a recorder to write their responses on sheets of butcher paper mounted on easels (or type them into the chat). Occasionally, participants leave all-day staff development sessions with their heads full of knowledge and their arms full of handouts. But they have missed out on opportunities to engage in meaningful conversations with other participants who have valuable insights to share about a common set of issues.

Throughout my career in administration, I have attended many workshops and conferences. Not all of them were as vacuous as the one described in the preceding paragraphs. One conference I attended was remarkable in comparison to others in which I have participated. This conference lasted an entire week, running from 8:30 a.m. to 3:30 p.m., and involved educators from all over the country. The gathering turned out to be a very positive and thought-provoking experience. Participants were given a thumb drive containing handouts and articles about the topics to be discussed.

The facilitators created groups representing small learning communities. Participants examined the information using techniques such as jigsaw, Socratic seminars, and collaborative assessment conferences. During the process, everyone had a seat at the table, and everyone's perspective was valued. Not only did the participants acquire the requisite knowledge base, but they also walked away with a set of process skills that could be used later to facilitate learning in their respective personal or professional settings.

As a bonus, workshop participants had a chance to develop a sense of trust and caring for those with whom they had shared the experience. In the trusting environment, their exchanges were much richer than they would have been among strangers. Together they created a situation in which they learned a great deal not only about the content but also about their colleagues. They enjoyed the privilege of hearing real-life stories about how certain ideas were or were not working in various settings. They got to know each other on a personal basis, and in this knowing, established mutual respect, even though they had come from diverse backgrounds and circumstances.

When group members walked away, they carried with them a sense of solidarity with the other participants. From the moment the community was established, the group experienced enrichment as a result of interacting with so many creative and experienced people who shared a concern. Workshop participants, that week, developed a sense of family, and as with most families, they vowed to stay in touch, support each other's efforts, and implement what they had learned.

During that week of community, small-group participants raised their awareness of the fact that no one person or group has the best and only right solution for challenging questions. They further discovered that the most effective "answers" do not come from an expert "out there." Rather, the expertise comes from within the group, where knowledge is constructed in a community with others. After pooling their collective and diverse savvy to explore important concerns they generated answers that are more likely to resemble "the truth" as it pertains to their particular situations. When the truth is derived through collaboration among participants who trust and respect one another, organizations can grow and change in positive ways.

Conducting Meetings with a Process Observer

Another useful skill for ministerial leaders is that of conducting meetings. A process observer can provide useful feedback as a means of helping the group improve its skills. This feedback takes the form of objective reflection that assists the group in becoming more effective. The process observer may be a member of the small group who steps outside the meeting space to record the data they have been asked to gather, or the observer can be any other respected person who has been asked to observe the group, record requested information, and provide feedback. Listed below are several components on which the process observer may focus. The group should agree on which criteria are to be observed; the process observer, then, will try to find examples of the presence or absence of each criterion.

1. The group's task is clear and deemed important by all members.
2. Group members feel free to express themselves.
3. Responsibilities involved in getting the work done are shared.
4. Actions to be taken are made clear and explicit.
5. Good communication skills are practiced.
6. The group periodically reviews how it goes about doing its work and makes adjustments where necessary.

The process observer serves as an evidence collector, not an evaluator. Based on the evidence collected, an assessment can be made of the process and progress of the meeting. The following list consists of questions that researchers have extracted from many such forms. Such checklists when used by a process observer can help members of the group become more effective participants.

Process Observer Checklist

Was the meeting slow in getting started?	Were there communication difficulties?
Was the atmosphere easy, relaxed, and comfortable?	Was there a feeling of giving and take?
Was the tempo slow, hurried, or satisfactory?	Were members eager to speak?
Was the interest level high? Was the purpose clear to all?	Were certain members taking more than their share of the time?
Was information shared? Was the discussion limited to the topic?	Were members assuming responsibility for the success of the meeting?
Were members sensitive to each other?	Were members attempting to draw out each other?
Were tensions brought out into the open?	Did the leader help the group to establish a direction?
Were ideas forced on the group?	Did the leader attempt to include nonparticipating members?
Was the group able to accept differences?	Was the group able to discipline itself?
Did the leader dominate the meeting?	Did the leader recognize those who wished to speak?
Was any decision reached?	Was there resistance to group decisions?
Was discussion centered for a long period in one portion of the group?	Did the leader bring the specialized skills to members to bear on the problem?
Did the leader summarize as necessary?	Did the leader get a consensus?

Decision-Making

Ministerial leaders should understand the steps involved in making effective decisions. Of course, all decision-making is bounded by the limitations of human rationality. No decision-making process, be it group or individual, is perfectly rational. Too many extraneous variables enter into the equation; and in the open systems environment, "perfection" is elusive, changing with the whims of the public, the extant political climate, and the financial realities associated with funding. What constitutes the most appropriate decision in one situation may not address the issues found in another climate and a different set of individuals.

Robert Owens reported that leaders can improve their decision-making behavior by sharpening their skills in logical, reflective thought. He noted that administrative reflective practices involve thinking that occurs simultaneously with managerial and administrative action. This kind of reflection grows out of uncertainty; when this occurs, the administrator constantly analyzes the situation, engaging in self-talk and questions designed to spark understanding, critical analysis, or alternative perspectives. According to Owens:

> *In that world, problem situations are experienced holistically, and the steps found in usual decision-making models are considered simultaneously rather than serially. This view suggests that emphasis on holistic thought-which seeks an understanding of the complexities, interconnections, ambiguities, and uncertainties of educational organizations-are more fruitful in decision making than the linear-and-step models proffered in the past.*[65]

Four Methods of Decision Making

Patterson and his colleagues described four basic methods for decision-making.[66] You may consider selecting among these options, depending on the situation you are in.

Command. These are decisions you make alone without involvement or counsel from anyone else. People tend to use this method when outside forces place demands on you that leave you with few options or when you plan to turn the decisions over other people and follow their lead.

Consult. With this method, you invite other people to provide their views on an issue before you make the final decision. Consulting with others can be "an efficient way of getting ideas and support without bogging down the decision-making process."[67]

Vote. When you are selecting from many good options, voting might be the appropriate option. Members have an opportunity to discuss the options before you call a vote. In the presence of quality choices, using voting may save time.

Consensus. With consensus, all members have a chance to contribute to the discussion with the understanding that their talk will bring them to a choice on which everyone can agree. While this method can produce unity in the organization, it is also time-consuming. The consensus method should be used only with high-stakes and complex issues or with issues where everyone must support the final choice.[68]

Steps for Making Successful Decisions

According to Saphier et al., making successful decisions involves twelve steps and three phases; namely, planning, deciding and implementing.[69]

Planning. Identify and explicitly state the issue, who owns it, and what the underlying goal is. Find out and explain how much discretion you have to take action or not. Must this issue be dealt with? State how strongly you feel about it. Every issue must land in someone's lap, to begin with. If it lands in yours, be sure to choose the proper path for who will make the preliminary and final decision from these options: An individual or group above you in the organization. You as administrator unilaterally. You as an administrator with input from staff. You as administrator and staff by consensus. Staff, with input from you as administrator. Staff by consensus. Staff by vote. A subgroup of staff, with input from others. A subgroup of staff unilaterally. Individual staff members unilaterally

At the beginning of the process, communicate clearly who will make the decision and identify any constraints that will affect the scope or content of the decision (i.e., staffing, budgeting, time). State explicitly the values you want to maintain and why they are not negotiable if that is the case. (For example, "Whatever proposals come forward, I want to hang on to small class size and that high quality of personal student-teacher contact we get from that.")

Deciding. Identify and periodically check out with members what the full impact or full consequences of the decision will be and communicate them to all parties involved. Involve all parties whose working conditions will be affected by the decision. Make clear the timeline for deciding and implementing the decision. Decide. Then make an explicit statement of the decision or recommendations, summarizing all key points. Provide exactly how and when the decision-making group will revisit the decision later to evaluate or revise it if necessary.

Implementing. Close the loop. Communicate the reasons for the decision fully and clearly to all affected parties after the decision is made, including how members' input was used. Plan how to monitor and support the day-to-day implementation of the decision and communicate these plans to everyone involved

Reaching Consensus

Because the current trend is to accept all voices as equal, it is important to find a way to mediate diverse viewpoints. This may be accomplished through a process of consensus building, which is collaborative. Consensus means a general agreement; judgment arrived at by most of those concerned; group solidarity in sentiment or belief. Many professionals who are responsible for facilitating group decision-making sessions understand further that consensus must be built on trusting relationships. Consensus is achieved informally (e.g., not arrived at through the "majority rules" procedure) and cannot be forced on participants. Rather, it is an affirmation of a particular decision-making group. For consensus to occur, a group must become a team or a fellowship – a community.

How does consensus-building work? The group needs to work together in positive ways to achieve mutual trust and understanding. The group is presented with a problem and is asked to solve to which each group member can agree. Members of the group assume that there will be differences of opinion based on the varying perspectives represented. Therefore, disagreement is taken for granted but not emphasized.

Brainstorming is one of the most productive and least personally threatening first steps the group takes together. In a brainstorming session many ideas, appropriate or not, are generated with no value judgments being made or expressed. The ideas are then considered, one by one, and those that are unworkable are discarded. Each person's point of view is sought and the meaning of each item they value is listened to find commonly held beliefs and values. There is a sense that once the person's meaning and point of view are truly understood, differences in beliefs will diminish or disappear.

The remaining ideas are considered, and rationales, both pro and con, are given. During this process, some group members may change their minds thereby bringing the group closer to consensus. Another possibility is that group members may suggest modifications of an idea that will satisfy those who did not approve of the idea in its original form. The group works within itself to agree on the most workable solutions.

Consensus is not always the appropriate process for decision-making. There are some situations in which a group may be providing information to an individual who decides because the individual is accountable for its consequences. In other situations, the individual given accountability for the decision may have data that cannot be shared with the group.

Problem Solving - Action Research

Effective decisions can grow out of action research, which is a systematic approach to investigation that begins with a problem, not a theory. Action research "proceeds inductively from experience to reflection" and onto action. "It embodies the principle of learning through doing, in which the skills of basic everyday problem-solving are transposed into a more structured, deliberative, and transparent process.[70] Because a range of perspectives from within the community is brought to bear on the issues under investigation, the actions that emanate from the collaboration have the potential to affect balance within the community ecology. The purpose of most action research is to "provide a place for the perspectives of members who have previously been marginalized from opportunities to develop and operate policies, programs, and services – perspectives often concealed by the products of a typical research process."[71] Graham further notes, this type of research contributes to "the increased well-being – economic, political, psychological, spiritual – of human persons and communities, and to a more equitable and sustainable relationship with the wider ecology of the planet of which we are an intrinsic part."

McIntyre[72] pinpointed three principles that guide most participatory action research projects: "(1) the collective investigation of a problem, (2) the reliance on indigenous knowledge to better understand that problem, and (3) the desire to take individual and/or collective action to deal with the stated problem. These aims are achieved through collective investigation, education, and action throughout the research process."

Additional characteristics of action research include collaboration among community members, focus on improving practice, decision-making driven by data, change in practice resulting from new awareness, and ongoing data collection and refinement. The process allows practitioners to become immersed in gathering evidence to support improvement in their day-to-day circumstances.[73]

Action researchers start with the simple premise that the situations under investigation are interfering with forwarding movement and members desire to find some way to improve them. Participants engage in collaborative processes to help them articulate how circumstances in their community are "produced, reproduced, and experienced daily."[74] To look at it from another perspective, collaborative action research engages a group of members in systematic trial and error. Hence, "all participants in the research process should rightfully be called researchers insofar as they engage in deliberate processes of inquiry or investigation with the intent of extending their understanding of a situation or a problem."[75]

The focus is on practice. Related questions include: How do we work with what we have to make our circumstances better than what they are now? How do we glean from our history and our surroundings the information we need to make better decisions? How do we raise our awareness of what is appropriate and activate a plan to make it happen? Through the use of participatory action research participants problematize issues of concern and position themselves as experts about their own lives.

Participatory action research engages participants in critical analysis, storytelling, historical research, statistics, and raising critical consciousness about the socio-cultural circumstances in the life of the organization. Action research works, in part, because a range of perspectives from within the community is brought to bear on the issues under investigation, and the actions that emanate from the collaboration have the potential to affect balance within the organizational ecology. The ability to engage in ongoing introspection empowers community members to take charge of their outcomes in ways that engender hope and self-determination.

Action research has the potential to change agents as well as agencies. Scrutiny of members, places, and circumstances may lead to modifications of viewpoint by requiring members to deconstruct rules, assumptions, and images; reflect on them, and reconstruct belief structures that enhance the organizational ecology.

THE MINISTER'S CODE OF ETHICS

I hope that everything in this book so far has reinforced the idea that if you practice effective ministerial leadership, you must also strive to lead in an ethical manner. The United Church of Christ, as well as other denominations, requires everyone with ministerial standing to abide by a ministerial code of ethics. The code uplifts the covenantal responsibilities of pastors toward God, self, family and the Church. Pastors who pay attention to the provisions of the code have respect for the well-being of both the organization and the people within it. They recognize ethical and moral boundaries associated with their leadership roles and take steps to be as sensitive as possible to the needs of the congregation and the community. Shown below is a bulleted list from the code of ethics for ministerial leaders in the United Church of Christ.[76]

- I will regard all persons with equal respect and concern and undertake to minister impartially.
- I will honor all confidences shared with me.
- I will not use my position, power, or authority to exploit any person.
- I will not use my position for personal financial gain, nor will I misuse the finances of the institution which I serve.

- I will not perform pastoral services within a parish or for a member of a parish without the consent of the pastor of that parish.
- I will deal honorably with the record of my predecessor and successor.
- I will not, upon my termination and departure from a ministry position, interfere with nor intrude upon the ministry of my successor.

Boundaries Training

To ensure that ministerial leaders are familiar with the Code of Ethics and possible violations of its provisions, all authorized ministers are required to attend boundaries training at least once every three years to maintain their standing. These trainings examine the nature of boundary issues and offer best practices for reducing the risk of boundary problems in the work setting. Typical learning objectives include the following:

- Define common boundary and ethics concepts as they relate to the human service field.
- Explore how relationships differ between themselves and their clients, co-workers, and supervisors.
- Evaluate the level of involvement in relationships at work.
- Assess risk of boundary-related issues at work and the harm these issues can create.
- Introduce strategies to prevent harm and what to do when risk is going up.

FaithTrust Institute

The FaithTrust Institute is one of many organizations offering boundaries training.[77] The Institute's curriculum and workshops aim to ensure that all faith and spiritual communities have resources to actively engage in prevention training. FaithTrust provides a structured curriculum for clergy and other spiritual leaders to help them create safe and healthy communities. Two of their offerings are Healthy Boundaries 101 and Healthy Boundaries 102. The 101 curriculum uses the DVD *A Sacred Trust*, which covers the following topics:

- Boundary Basics for Clergy and Teachers
- Dating, Friendships, Gifts, and Dual Relationships
- Transference and Touch Boundaries
- Emerging Issues: Social Media and Technology
- Personal Needs and Self-Care: Personal and Professional Health

The curriculum for 201 uses both *A Sacred Trust*, as well as *Once You Cross the Line*. The 201 curriculum offers advanced training for ministerial leaders who are already familiar with the basic content of healthy boundaries. Session topics for 201 include:

- Joy of Boundaries: Revisiting the Basics and Developing a Deeper Understanding
- Theology and Boundaries
- Power and Vulnerability
- Boundaries and Internet Technology
- Boundaries and Social Media
- Boundaries and Finance
- Boundaries and Attraction
- Self-Care

FORTITYING ETHICAL BEHAVIOR THROUGH CASE STUDIES

Most people have crossed boundaries at some point in life, either knowingly or unknowingly. Sometimes these transgressions occur because of lack prior of knowledge or lack of experience in recognizing when and where limitations on behavior should be imposed. At every stage of human interaction, effective ministerial leaders are obligated to make informed decisions based on sound ethical principles. One author noted that understanding the factors involved in making responsible ethical decisions takes time and practice.

Case studies provide an effective way to learn from vicarious experience. Michael R. Milco observed that today's pastors have to face what he calls "a multifaceted ethical maze." He provides a series of ethical dilemmas in church leadership in the form of case studies that employ a decision-making tool based on biblical principles. He calls the tool the Decision-Making Tower, which consists of four levels of analysis. At level one, the model calls on you to describe the **dilemma** and asks, "what happened?" For level two, the question is, "How do my **personal values** impact my understanding?" Level three deals with principles in response to the questions, "What **principles** strongly guide my life? What theological framework am I applying?" At level four, the probing, questions are, "How does my **personality** factor into the way I interpret certain events," and "What external factors influence me?" Milco concludes:

> *"My desire is that we consciously consider each level in the Decision-Making Tower in order to understand the dynamics in the decision-making process. In addition to considering each level carefully, the Decision-Making Tower must be viewed as an organic whole, a flow of elements that continually interacts among the four levels. The only two constants are the dilemma and the decision, while our principles, values, and loyalties are synthesized in the process."[78]*

Milco's decision-based analysis framework remains valid in most situations we encounter today. Some of his cases, however, may seem dated by today's standards. Nevertheless, they can help you practice your analytical skills and sharpen your ethical awareness. His book is listed as a resource at the end of this chapter.

MAINTAINING HEALTHY BOUNDARIES

The preceding chapters have discussed skills, behaviors, and dispositions of effective ministerial leaders. You learned from your reading that these leaders engage in ethical behavior and understand the need for appropriate boundaries. Specifically, effective ministerial leaders understand the nature of their call, have the ability to manage change, engage in theological reflection, prepare for worship, care for self, and engage in effective teaching and learning around a variety of sensitive issues and social concerns. These leaders understand the principles and practices of cross-cultural communication. They are aware of various leadership styles and adjust their practices to fit unique challenges and situations. They are good administrators with skills in staff development, decision making, and problem solving. Additionally, effective ministerial leaders are able to articulate the mission, vision, and core values of the organization and implement plans to meet the needs of the people they serve. Not only that; the effective ministerial leader performs all these responsibilities in an ethical manner that facilitates organizational well-being. Developing skill in the ministerial leadership dispositions identified in this book may raise your awareness about practices that help you maintain healthy boundaries.

WORKSHOP EXERCISES

8:30 a.m. – 9:00 a.m.	Invocation/Welcome Introductions/Community Building Creating a Hospitable Environment
9:00 a.m. – 12:00 noon	**Workshop Session 1: Overview** **Activity 1 – Experiential Learning** **Activity 2 – Case Writing**
12:30 p.m. – 1:00 p.m.	Lunch
2:00 p.m. – 5:00 p.m.	**Workshop Session 2** **Activity 1 – Case Analysis** **Activity 2 – Consultancy Protocol**
5:30 p.m. – 6:00 p.m.	Workshop Evaluation Closing Worship, Benediction, Dismissal

Learning Activity: Experiential Learning
Think about your unique setting. Briefly describe an experience you had or observed involving failure to maintain healthy boundaries. What was troubling about the experience? In what ways could the principles described in this book have mitigated the situation?

Learning Activity: Case Study Writing
Write up a case of congregational or clergy misconduct that you have observed or come to know as a result of reliable information (800-1000 words). Keep the identities of all parties, including the name of the church and location, confidential by using pseudonymous. Include these elements in your case:
- What happened?
- What are the relevant ethical principles? Were any of these principles apparent to the people involved? Were the principles known but ignored? Was it an opportunity for moral guidance by the minister? Did

the minister or other leadership accept their moral
leadership role?
- How did the involved parties respond to the event?
- What was the outcome? Was it a teaching/ learning
  moment for involved parties and/or the church?

Case Analysis: "Surrender"
The Holy Providence Christian Center attracted people from
near and far to hear the message of the new pastor, Rev. Richard
L. Wilson. He gave the people what they wanted to hear, and
they came in droves. As a result, the church on Laodicea Street
was one of the fastest growing in the city, with more members
now than the populations of many small towns. And so,
Hannah had come. She had come today searching for serenity,
seeking refuge once again, after years of wandering. She had
come to claim hope. But when Hannah finally reached the
pastor's office, her heart sank. Rev. Wilson was out of town.
Out of desperation, she agreed instead to talk to Rev. Dawson,
one of the elderly assistant pastors. He had no pastoral
counseling training or experience, but he decided he would
counsel Hannah anyway.

Now awkward and thrown off guard, Hannah took a seat
in the office as the pastor closed the door. Nervous, Hannah
stumbled to find the words to convey her version of that which
had made her life a living hell. She sat on the edge of her chair
as if leaning forward would help her express her angst – she had
been emotionally and physically flogged by her spouse and
generally battered by her life. She was in dire need of a
prescription to make the pain go away.

The Rev. Dawson sat across the desk from her with his
hands in a steeple position. He leaned back in his chair and
studied her while she talked. The tapping of his foot distracted
Hannah as she tried to weave the threads of her saga into
something the reverend could understand. Perhaps she wasn't

making much sense. Maybe she wasn't speaking loudly enough or clearly enough. Perhaps she had rambled on too long. But, in the middle of one of her statements, Rev. Dawson interrupted her. He spoke up as if he had received a revelation which preempted anything she could possibly have to say.

So, she stopped talking. As he began to speak, expectancy cloyed the air.

"I really don't know you, Sister Chambers. And I don't have much experience in all of that counseling stuff," the reverend announced. "But I can tell you this. When you go home tonight, you need to pray for your marriage. Ask God to show you how to be a good wife. Ask him to give you more patience and strength to get you through this rough patch. Let me ask you this – What have you done to provoke your husband lately?"

Hannah was stunned. *"My very existence provokes him.... Are you deaf?"* Her thoughts screamed. In silence, she glared at him.

"Well, Sister Chambers, the Bible says wives should submit to their husbands." He continued. "Under no circumstances should you break your marriage vows. Just keep on looking to the Lord so you can receive your joy in heaven. ...Now let us pray."

While he prayed, her thoughts raced. Never once did the reverend ask her if she was safe or if she needed medical help. Not once did he ask her if she had a place to go in the event she couldn't go home. He laid the blame firmly on her shoulders as he dismissed her feelings and trivialized her plight. The burden was almost more than she could bear. The words and thoughts went on and on.

Finally, in unison, they said "Amen."

He shook her hand. His grasp was weak. "God bless you, Sister Chambers," the reverend said as he turned away from her quickly and directed his attention to a stack of papers on his desk.

Battling hysteria, Hannah couldn't decide whether to laugh or cry. How was she supposed to follow someone who had no idea where he was headed? How was she to submit to a man who paraded his paramours shamelessly in her face? How was she to love this man who loved only himself? She stumbled out of the assistant pastor's office and into the chapel across the hall. There, she collapsed onto one of the pews. Her sobs erupted from a place so deep inside her that they wracked her chest cavity and tore past her throat.

She sat there a long time; the church staff having the good sense to leave her alone. Gradually, she became aware of her surroundings. The room was dimly lit. Rows of pecan wooden benches filled the sanctuary. Their stiff cushions, upholstered in red and purple, scratched her skin and kept her in touch with her pain. Red carpet lined the aisles leading to the pulpit, which had a stained-glass window as its backdrop. The colored glass partially masked a baptismal pool. Hannah sat back in the pew and closed her eyes. She rocked herself back and forth. The only sound in the room was the whisper of lapping water.

"Can you see me, God?" She prayed. Officially tired – worn out in every way a woman could be weary – she ached for relief. The water whispered. "Can you hear me, Holy Spirit?" Hannah pleaded.

Before long, the water's voice engulfed her psyche and wrapped its peacefulness around her soul. The dull ache in her body subsided while her chest rose and fell to the rhythm of the wash.

Case Questions:

Using the four levels of Michael R. Milco's Decision-Making Tower, analyze the case presented above from the perspective of Rev. Dawson. At level one, the model calls on you to describe the **dilemma** and asks, "What happened?" For level two, the question is, "How do **personal values** impact the reverend's understanding?" Level three deals with the scenario in response to the questions, "What **principles** strongly guide the pastor's life? What theological frameworks is Rev. Dawson applying?" At level four, the probing, questions are, "How does the reverend's **personality** factor into the way he interprets the events," and "What external factors influence Rev. Dawson? Now take it one step further. If you were the pastor in this case, what would you do?

Learning Activity: The Consultancy Protocol

A consultancy is a structured process for promoting clear thinking about a problem or dilemma. Ministerial leaders may use this tool to clarify issues related to possible violations of the code of ethics. My initial exposure to this powerful tool was when I worked as a consultant for urban education. According to the developers, the protocol has two main purposes. First, it helps participants improve their capacity to see and describe the dilemmas pertaining to their work by bringing in outside perspectives. Second, it helps participants understand the depth of the issues and make suggestions to deal with them.[79]

The consultancy requires about 45 to 55 minutes to complete.   Participants will assume different roles: the presenter, whose problem is being discussed by the group, and the facilitator, who also participates if the group is small.

Step 1: The presenter gives an overview of the dilemma or problem. They highlight the major issues of the problem then frames a question for the consultancy group to consider. This step works best when the presenter's reflection is clear and thorough, and the quality of the question lends itself to further exploration. (5 minutes)

Step 2: The consultancy group asks clarifying questions of the presenter. These should be questions that have brief and factual answers. (5 minutes)

Step 3: The group then asks probing questions of the presenter. The questions should be worded so that they enhance the questioner's clarify and expand the questioner's thinking about the dilemma that has been presented to the consultancy group. The goal here is for the questioner to learn more about the question or to do some analysis of the presented dilemma. she presented. While the presenter responds to the group's questions, there is no discussion by the larger group of the presenter's responses. (10 minutes)

Step 4: The group then talks with each other about the presented dilemma. What did you hear? What didn't you hear that you think might be relevant? What do you think about the problem? Members of the group sometimes suggest solutions to the dilemma. Usually, however, they work to define the issues more thoroughly and objectively. The presenters are not allowed to speak during this discussion, but instead listen and take notes. (15 minutes)

Step 5: The presenter then responds to the discussion (first in a fishbowl if there is more than one presenter and if they prefer to begin that way), followed by a whole group discussion. One facilitator leads a conversation about the group's observation of the process. (5 minutes)

Step 6: Debrief the consultancy process. What worked? What didn't work? What was learned? (5 minutes)

Those who wish to use this protocol for tackling dilemmas should consider the following implementation tips:

Step 1: The success of the consultancy often depends on the quality of the presenter's reflection in Step 1, as well as on the quality and authenticity of the question framed for the consultancy group. However, it is not uncommon for the presenter, at the end of a consultancy, to say, "Now I know what my real question is." That is fine, too. It is sometimes helpful for the presenter to prepare ahead of time a brief (one-two page) written description of the dilemma and the issues related to it for the consultancy group to read as part of Step 1.

Steps 2 & 3: Clarifying questions are for the person asking them. They ask the presenter "who, what, where, when, and how." These are not "why' questions. They can be answered quickly and succinctly, often with a phrase or two. Probing questions are for the person answering them. They ask the presenter "why" (among other things), and are open-ended. They take longer to answer, and often require deep thought on the part of the presenter before she speaks.

Step 4: When the group talks while the presenter listens, it is helpful for the presenter to pull her chair back slightly away from the group. This protocol requires the consultancy group to talk about the presenter in the third person, almost as if she is not there. As awkward as this may feel at first, it often opens up a rich conversation. Remember that it is the group's job to offer an analysis of the dilemma or question presented. It is not necessary to solve, the dilemma or to offer a definitive answer. It Is important for the presenter to listen in a non-defensive manner. Listen for new ideas, perspectives, and approaches. Listen to the group's analysis of your questions or issues. Listen for assumptions -- both your own and the group's-implicit in the conversation. Don't listen for judgment of you by the group. This is not supposed to be about you, but about a question you have raised. Remember chat you asked the group to help you with this dilemma.

Step 5: The point of this time period is not for the presenter to give a 'blow by blow' response to the group's conversation, nor is it to defend or further e.-.plain herself Rather, this is a time for the presenter to talk about what were, for her, the most significant comments, ideas and questions she heard. She can also share any new thoughts or questions she had while listening to the consultancy group.

Consultancy Protocol Practice Activity: Recall an ethical dilemma you have encountered or heard about recently. Form a group to demonstrate use of the consultancy protocol as a structured process for promoting clear thinking about the problem or dilemma.

Learning Activity: Reflect on the best staff development workshop you ever attended. Identify the elements that made it exceptional. Discuss how you would structure a workshop for your ministerial setting.

Action Research: Identify a problem in your ministerial setting that could be addressed through action research. Discuss how you would carry out the research process in your setting.

Personal Experiences: Now think about your unique setting. Briefly describe an experience you had involving administrative duties. What was rewarding about the experience? What was challenging?

SUGGESTED RESOURCES

"Case Studies for Analysis:" Milco, Michael R. (1997). *Ethical dilemmas in church leadership: Case studies in biblical decision-making.* Grand Rapids, MI: Kregel Publications.

"Ordained Minister's Code." Available at: https://www.ucc.org/what-we-do/justice-local-church-ministries/local-church/mesa-ministerial-excellence-support-and-authorization/ministers/ministers_ordained-ministers-code/

"Ethical Standards and Standards of Practice for Ministry Personnel." Available at: https://united-church.ca/sites/default/files/ethical-standards-practice-ministry-personnel.pdf

"United Church of Christ, Manual on Ministry." Available at: https://www.uccfiles.com/pdf/ManualonMinistry-2018.pdf

Intersection of Perspective Transformation and Action Research

Phases of Transformation	Steps of Action Research
1. Disorienting dilemma	Realized Need To Change
2. Self-examination	**Step 1: Look - Build a picture.**
3. Critical assessment of assumptions	**Step 2: Think.** Interpret and explain what you see. Ask interpretive questions - Who, What, Where, When, Why, and How?
4. Recognizing link between discontent and the desire to transformation	Prepare to fine-tune the problem. What is real? What is ideal? What is the desired compromise?
5. Exploration of options	Define tasks required to address the problem. Chart the course and explore options.
6. Planning a course of action	**Step 3: Act.** Move forward. Formulate a detailed implementation plan. Identify task, steps, people, places, times, materials, and funds.
7. Acquiring knowledge and skills	Reflect. Evaluate and interpret data: What new knowledge have you gained? What has been the impact on the issue of concern? What do you still need to know?
8. Provisional trying of new roles	Test options.
9. Building competence and self-confidence	Identify additional training needs. What additional training is required to build competence in the new role or situation?
10. Reintegration into one's life of conditions dictated by one's new perspective	Internalize/Institutionalize your plans. Develop new vision, routines, policies, and procedures to sustain the new outcome.

Chapter 10: Planning Strategically

CHAPTER PREVIEW

Readings and exercises in this chapter will help you:
- Assess the long-range needs of your setting.
- Formulate a strategic plan.
- Develop an action plan.

THE IMPORTANCE OF STRATEGIC PLANNING

At some point in your ministerial career, you might want to engage in a process that examines your organization's values, current status, and environment, and then relate these factors to the organization's desired future state. This process, called strategic planning, addresses three questions: (a) Who are we? (b) Where are we going? (c) How will we get there?[80]

The strategic planning process begins with a belief statement and a vision of what the community should be, then provides a framework that guides choices related to the future nature and direction of the community. The end product is usually expressed in terms of a five-year or ten-year plan. Using input from the internal and external community as a barometer, you can use the process to gain new, and perhaps better, information to support decisions related to sustained growth. The literature varies on the precise number and nature of components that should be included in strategic planning. The following list encompasses the most commonly cited steps in the process.

Assessing the External Environment

During this phase of the process, you will typically identify threats that might impede the accomplishment of your mission and pinpoint opportunities for collaboration among members of the community. Among the factors that should be examined, you should include the economic, demographic, social, technological, and political concerns that may have implications for the community's future. Methods for gathering information about the external environment include surveys, interviews, the key informant technique, community forums, and other mechanisms.

Assessing Internal Capacity

Because your community is unique, you will want to do some self-examination to sort through the varying perspectives that parishioners and supporters bring to the table. During the internal analysis, you and your planning team will identify strengths and weaknesses existing in the targeted community. Factors you should examine include church governance, culture, leadership, staff expertise, commitment, Christian educational curriculum, and congregational characteristics, and others. In addition, the planning team will conduct community-wide informational meetings to outline goals, objectives, and activities for incorporation into an integrated action plan.

Mission/Vision Driven Focus

Every viable plan for change should include a clearly defined mission and vision that serve as the driving force behind everything that takes place in your organization. They serve as the umbrella under which all other activities will occur. Your mission and vision constitute the mutually defined, commonly shared purposes for the existence of the organization with a future-oriented sense of what it is capable of becoming. Together, the mission and vision provide coherence for the work you will accomplish.

Mission

Your mission is your organization's long-term statement of purpose that identifies the scope of its operations and reflects organizational values and priorities. The purpose of a mission statement is to help the organization make consistent decisions, motivate, build organizational unity, integrate short-term objectives with longer-term goals, and enhance communication. The mission statement must have a target audience and must keep this audience in mind as you and your committee drafted components of the mission.

You should make sure your mission statement is relatively brief and easily remembered. A good mission statement should include particular characteristics. For example, the format of the mission statement should be suitable for framing, wallet-sized cards, or anything else in between. The statement should be long enough to reach the target audience: one sentence to one page. The mission statement should be designed to last many years, but the organization should not be afraid to rewrite the mission when it becomes necessary because of changing circumstances. The language used in the mission statement should be selected to appeal to the target audience, but each word in the mission statement should be selected deliberately.

Vision

As the ministerial leader in your setting, you must recognize the importance of organizational vision. It is this vision that drives what occurs in the organization and your actions that determine whether the organization will move forward smoothly. Your vision will set the mood and the tone for daily activities. The organizational vision will serve as the shared frame of reference that serves as the guide for everything that follows. After the vision is formulated, you will have to be the keeper of collective vision, editor, cheerleader, problem solver, and resource finder.

The organizational vision will be developed in conjunction with the community and will address the long-term hopes and dreams of what the organization can become. The ministerial leader might start by asking community planners to brainstorm about the characteristics of the ideal organization. Ask them to compare their present status to the ideal. In doing so, you and your planning committee can identify several gaps between the real and the ideal. Further discussions will lead to the identification of ways to bridge the gaps. Provided on the next page is an example of a mission and vision statement I helped to develop for a regional continuing education program.

Core Values

Your mission/vision statement should reinforce the organization's core values. Core values are "the constant, passionate, biblical core beliefs that go deep and really, truly empower and guide the ministry."[81]

The bulleted list below provides a sample of core values expressed by the region, which is committed to incorporating their core values in all that they do. They aim to:

- Practice deep spiritual formation exemplified by acceptance and forgiveness, Christ-centered, God-honoring praxis, and commitment to the Gospel of Jesus.
- Practice meaningful trusting relationships marked by authenticity, honesty, integrity, trustworthiness, collaborative approaches to learning, not harming, emphasis on diversity, inclusivity, and kindness.
- Practice covenantal connections with our ministerial partners.
- Practice pro-reconciliation/anti-racism by emphasizing multicultural awareness, justice, and racial equity.
- Practice creative ministry is characterized by excellence, critical thinking and problem solving, collaboration, and experiential learning.

Sample Mission and Vision Statements

Mission – To cultivate excellence in ministry marked by positive ethics and personal integrity.

Vision – We strive to empower clergy, as life-long learners, to pursue, demonstrate, and articulate ethical ideals, culturally sensitive collaboration, and conscientious leadership in the Region's rapidly changing and demographically diverse congregational and non-congregational environments.

Our course offerings aim to address the needs of adult learners through an articulated ethics curriculum. We strive to foster critical thinking, effective communication, and creativity, along with the ability to sustain effective and ethical relationships in evolving congregational and non-congregational settings.

We endeavor to create an environment in which learners and facilitators work together collaboratively, proactively, and reflectively to explore ideas and opportunities related to diversity, equity, inclusivity, personal and professional ethics, and social justice within the church community and beyond.

Our programs, policies, and practices reinforce the Region's commitment to be an inclusive church community that embraces all seekers, including members with multiracial, multiethnic and LGBTQ+ identities. Our praxis reinforces the core values of the region and encourages adherence to ethical practices for self-care, principled financial management, appropriate sexual conduct, and pro-reconciliation/anti-racism ideals among all clergy.

Establishing Goals, Objectives, and Action Plans

After you have identified your mission, vision, and values, setting goals and objectives is the next step in the process. Your goals will emerge by examining what is to be achieved and in what order. Your specific objectives will grow out of this activity and will represent smaller, observable, and measurable steps toward accomplishing the goals. Your action plans can be even more detailed, in that they specify what will occur, who will be responsible, how will it take place, and when will it be done.

Identifying Funding Sources

Your strategic plan should contain a budget that reflects priorities to help the organization achieve the stated mission and realize the goals. The budget represents a commitment by the community to fulfill the provisions of the plan. It responds to the query, "How much of our time, talent, testimonies, and treasures will we need to accomplish the mission?" The budget translates the community's priorities into financial and action terms within the context of available resources. Once it has been approved, the budget establishes the basis for all spending within the organization.

Gap Analysis

Gap analysis forces planners to examine the space separating the ideal from the real and to identify ways of bridging the gap between the two. It is a fairly simple process. You will gather data during this phase by using interviews, observations, questionnaires, and other tools. The gap analysis document can also be used to track simple goals to help you determine where you are in relation to where you want to be. Pinpointing patterns in the data will reveal critical issues, which will then serve as the basis for establishing goals, objectives, and action plans. You may summarize your findings using the template below.

Developing an Action Plan

Your action plan will detail observable and measurable activities in which the organization will engage to address the objectives that have been identified. The plan will also specify the time frame in which the activities are to occur, the persons responsible for coordinating the activities, the indicators of successful accomplishment of objectives, and the costs associated with each activity.

The organizational governing board should have an opportunity to review the drafted action plan and to provide their feedback before final approval. Keep in mind that it usually is not enough to assume that everyone shares a common understanding of where the organization is headed and how it is going to get there.

You should evaluate your plan periodically. Some elements of the evaluation plan will include conducting monthly reviews to assess "what's working" and "what needs to be changed," establishing opportunities for members to attend professional development workshops or webinars periodically to share success stories and learn about best practices, and to celebrate successes as a group.

Implementing the Plan

Most of the activities in your action plan will be short-term in duration and can be monitored to ensure they are completed according to the timelines established. Not only that, but the action plan also identifies members who will take the lead on completing each action step. In the long run, if all steps are followed as planned or if adjustments are made to account for unforeseen events, the community will be able to move systematically toward its goals

WORKSHOP EXERCISES

8:30 a.m. – 9:00 a.m.	Invocation/Welcome Introductions/Community Building Creating a Hospitable Environment
9:00 a.m. – 12:00 noon	**Workshop Session 1** **Activity 1 – Assess Environment** **Activity 2 – Identify Mission** **Activity 3 – Clarify Vision** **Activity 4 – Establish Core Values**
12:30 p.m. – 1:00 p.m.	Lunch
2:00 p.m. – 5:00 p.m.	**Workshop Session 2** **Activity 1 – Establish Goals/Obj.** **Activity 2 - Perform Gap Analysis** **Activity 3 – Action Planning**
5:30 p.m. – 6:00 p.m.	Workshop Evaluation Closing Worship, Benediction, Dismissal

Learning Activity: Identify the Mission, Vision, Values
Using a consensus-building framework is an effective way to generate a large number of ideas in a short time. The ideas can be considered, one by one, and those that are unworkable are discarded. Each person's point of view is sought and the meaning of each item they value is listened to find commonly held beliefs and values. Our topic of interest is identifying desired mission, vision, and values of the organization.
Consensus Building
Use the process outlined below to identify the mission of the organization. The process may be repeated for the vision and values. The process is outlined below. :

- Brainstorming - generate as long a list as possible of what you consider to be important core values.

- In small groups (3 to 5 people) review the brainstormed list and select the three most desirable and the three least desirable statements on the list. (Report)
- In larger group, compare the small group lists. (Discuss)
- Discuss the items and determine the 5-7 most important values.

Learning Activity: Establish Goals/Objectives
Use this process to identify the goals and objectives of the organization.
- Brainstorming - generate as long a list as possible of what you consider to be important core values.
- In small groups (3 to 5 people) review the brainstormed list and select the three most desirable and the three least desirable statements on the list. (Report)
- In larger group, compare the small group lists. (Discuss)
- Discuss the items and determine the 5-7 most important values.

Learning Activity: Gap Analysis
- Imagine that you have the task of developing a gap analysis and action plan for your strategic planning process. Describe the steps you will take to complete the task.
- What is the organizational ideal you want to attain? How does your existing situation differ from your ideal?
- Discuss various alternatives for closing the gap between the real and ideal, and make a note of the

challenges you might encounter in closing the gaps.
Compare your situation to that of your groupmates.

Gap Analysis Template

Area of Analysis:				
Goal for Analysis:				
Ideal (desired situation)	Real (Existing situation)	The gap in real and ideal	What is needed to reduce the gap?	Issues and risks

Learning Activity: Action Planning

After your analysis, it is time to develop an action plan. You may use the template below to guide your work.

Timeline

Task	Begin	End	Responsible

Learning Activity: Budgeting
The group should formulate a draft budget, taking into account the items listed in the spreadsheet below.

Item	Explanation	Amount
Travel/ Lodging		
Contractual Services		
Equipment		
Software		
Data Entry/and Clerical		
Telecommunications		
Training and Education		
Other Commodities		
Indirect Costs		

Experience:
Now think about your unique setting. Briefly describe an experience you had involving strategic planning or other forms of planning. What was rewarding about the experience? What was challenging?

SUGGESTED RESOURCES

"Example of a Five-Year Growth Action Plan for the Billing Parish Church." Available at:
http://www.billing.church/sites/default/files/attachments/pdf/Billing%20Growth%20Action%20Plan%202018.pdf

Aubrey Malphurs. (2013). *Advanced Strategic Planning: A 21st-Century Model for Church and Ministry Leaders* **Paperback (3rd ed.).** Ada, MI: Baker Books.

Lorrie C. Reed

APPENDICES

Appendix A: United Church of Christ Marks of Faithful and Effective Authorized Ministers

The United Church of Christ has outlined Marks of Faithful and Effective Authorized Ministers In the United Church Of Christ.[82] These Marks represent competencies ministerial leaders should possess. According to the Manual on Ministry: "the Marks strive to highlight the complex combination of talents, understandings, and skills needed for ministerial leadership in the United Church of Christ. Committees on Ministry are guided in their work of authorizing and overseeing Ordained Ministers by the Marks of Faithful and Effective Authorized Ministers."[83] The listing below presents eight marks of effectiveness along with bullet points for each item.

Exhibiting A Spiritual Foundation and Ongoing Spiritual Practice

- Loving God, following Jesus Christ, and being guided by the Holy Spirit, living a life of discipleship.
- Praying actively and nurturing spiritual practices.
- Being called to ordained ministry by God and the Church.
- Continuing discernment of one's call in community.
- Understanding the power of the Holy Spirit at work through the elements of Christian worship to nurture faith.
- Exhibiting a commitment to lifelong spiritual development and faithful personal stewardship.

Nurturing UCC Identity

- Acknowledging Jesus Christ as the sole Head of the Church.
- Communicating passion for the oneness of the Body of Christ (John 17:21).

- Holding active membership in a Local Church of the United Church of Christ.
- Participating in the various settings of the United Church of Christ, including Local
- Churches, Associations, Conferences, General Synod, and global ministries.
- Knowing and appreciating UCC history, polity, and theology.
- Exhibiting a commitment to the core values of the United Church of Christ: continuing testament, extravagant welcome, and changing lives.

Building Transformational Leadership Skills

- Empowering the Church to be faithful to God's call, reflective of Christ's mission, and open to the surprises of the Holy Spirit.
- Strategically creating the future of God's Church.
- Witnessing in the public square to God's redeeming power.
- Performing necessary and appropriate administrative tasks.
- Working collaboratively with intercultural awareness and sensitivity.
- Encouraging leadership development of self and others through continuing education and lifelong learning.

Engaging Sacred Stories and Traditions

- Exhibiting knowledge, understanding, and continuing study of the Hebrew Scriptures and the New Testament.
- Maturing in effective proclamation and preaching.
- Understanding the history of the Christian Church, from biblical times forward.

- Bringing life to sacred stories and traditions in worship, proclamation, and witness.
- Leading faith formation effectively across generations.
- Holding the Holy with integrity especially as represented in the Sacraments.

Caring for All Creation

- Nurturing care and compassion for God's creation.
- Maintaining a basic understanding of mental health and wellness.
- Practicing self-care and life balance.
- Providing hope and healing to a hurting world.
- Attending to one's own spiritual and pastoral care, including engagement in supervision as appropriate.
- Stewarding the resources of the Church.

Participating in Theological Praxis

- Practicing theological reflection and engagement as part of one's sense of ministerial
- identity.
- Integrating theological reflection in teaching, preaching, and ecclesial and community leadership.
- Articulating a theology and practice of ministry consistent with the UCC Manual on Ministry.
- Demonstrating an appreciation for and participation in the ecumenical and interfaith partnerships of the UCC.
- Experiencing and appreciating a variety of theological perspectives.
- Embodying the UCC Ministerial Code.

Working Together for Justice And Mercy

- Drawing on the ministry of Jesus Christ to confront injustice and oppression.

- Practicing the radical hospitality of God.
- Identifying and working to overcome explicit and implicit bias in the life of the Church.
- Understanding community context and navigating change with a community.
- Engaging in mission and outreach.
- Building relationships of mutual trust and interdependence.

Strengthening Inter- and Intra- Personal Assets
- Developing and maintaining a healthy sense of self as shaped by God, community, and life experiences.
- Living in relationships of covenantal accountability with God and the Church.
- Exhibiting strong moral character and personal integrity.
- Respecting the dignity of all God's people.
- Understanding and ministering to stages of human development across the life span.
- Demonstrating excellent communication skills.

Appendix B: A Selected Bibliography for Teaching about Racial Justice

Alexander, M. (2020). *The new Jim Crow: Mass incarceration in the age of colorblindness.* New York: New Press.

Barber, W. (2020). *We are called to be a movement.* New York: Workman Publishing Co.

Barber, W. J., & Wilson-Hartgrove, J. (2016). *The third reconstruction: How a moral movement is overcoming the politics of division and fear.* Boston, MA: Beacon Press.

Cone, J. (2013). *The cross and the lynching tree.* Maryknoll, NY: Orbis Books.

Davis, F. E. (2019). *The little book of race and restorative justice: Black lives, healing, and us social transformation (justice and peacebuilding).* New York: Good Books.

DeWolf, T. N., & Geddes, J. (2019). *The little book of racial healing: Coming to the table for truth-telling, liberation, and transformation (justice and peacebuilding).* New York: Good Books.

DiAngelo, R. (2018). *White fragility: Why it's so hard for white people to talk about racism.* Boston, MA: Beacon Press.

DuBois, W.E.B. (1998). *Black reconstruction in America, 1860-1880.* New York: The Free Press.

DuBois, W.E.B., Douglass, F., & Washington, B.T. (2007). *Three African-American classics: Up from slavery, The souls of black folk and Narrative of the life of Frederick Douglass.* New York: Dover Publications.

Freire, P. (1970, 2000). *Pedagogy of the oppressed.* New York, NY: Continuum.

Grant, J. (1989). *White women's Christ and Black women's Jesus: Feminist Christology and womanist response (AAR Academy Series)* 1st Edition. Atlanta, GA: American Academy of Religion.

Hooker, D. A. (2016). *The little book of transformative community conferencing: A hopeful, practical approach to dialogue (justice and peacebuilding).* New York: Good Books.

Jones, R. P. (2020). *White too long: The legacy of white supremacy in American Christianity.* New York: Simon & Schuster.

King, M. L., Jr. (2010). *Strength to love.* Minneapolis, MN: Augsburg Fortress Press.

Manakem, R. (2017). *My grandmother's hands: Racialized trauma and the pathway to mending our hearts and bodies.* Las Vegas, NV: Central Recovery Press.

Mezirow, J. (1991, 2009). *Transformative dimensions of adult learning* (Kindle Edition). San Francisco: Jossey-Bass.

Mezirow, J. (1997). Transformative learning: Theory to practice. *New Directions For Adult & Continuing Education, 1997*(74), 5.

Patterson, Kerry, Grenny, Joseph, McMillan, Ron, and Switzler, Al. (2012). Crucial Conversations: Tools for Talking When Stakes are High (2nd edition). New York: McGraw Hill.

Peacock, B. L. (2020). *Soul care in African American practice.* Downers Grove, IL: Intervarsity Press.

Tatum, B. D. (2017). *Why are all the Black kids sitting together in the cafeteria?: And other conversations about race.* New York: Basic Books.

Thurman, H. (1996). *Jesus and the disinherited.* Boston, MA: Beacon Press.

Wilkerson, I. (2011). *The warmth of other suns: The epic story of America's great migration.* New York: Vintage Books.

Wilkerson, I. (2020). *Caste: The origins of our discontents.* New York: Random House.

Winters, Mary Frances. 2020. Inclusive conversations: fostering equity, empathy, and belonging across differences. Oakland, CA: Berrett-Koehler Publishers, Inc.

Woodson, C. G. (2010). *The Mis-education of the Negro.* New York: SoHo Books.

Appendix C: Workshop Evaluation Form

Instructions: *Please evaluate your workshop experiences by placing a checkmark in the box that corresponds with your opinion. SD=strongly disagree, D=Disagree, A=Agree, SA=Strongly agree, NA=Not applicable to you. Your responses are anonymous. Space is provided at the end of this form for additional comments. We value your honest input!*

#		SD	D	A	SA	NA	Other
1.	Materials/handouts were helpful.						
2.	The workshop facilitated my discernment.						
3.	The workshop provided sufficient opportunities for interaction.						
4.	During the workshop, I had opportunities to bond with colleagues.						
5.	Activities consisted of a good balance between contemplative and active exercises.						
6.	The workshop helped me think critically about the issues.						
7.	The workshop increased my understanding of ministerial leadership.						

Lorrie C. Reed

Workshop Evaluation Open-ended Item

8. Please comment on any aspect of the workshop.

About the Author

Lorrie C. Reed, M. Div., Ph.D., is the former Executive Director of the School for Ministry, a collaborative program for preparation of lay ministerial leaders. She is ordained as a minister in the United Church of Christ. Dr. Reed's professional experiences include service as a secondary school teacher, high school associate principal, middle school principal, curriculum director, university professor, and consultant. She is the former Associate Pastor for Christian Education at a United Church of Christ congregation in the Chicago metropolitan area and the founder of Rivertree Christian Chapel, an online ministry.

Dr. Reed is the author of several books and holds a Ph.D. in Research Methodology, a master's degree in Educational Administration, a master's degree in Theological Studies, a Master of Divinity degree, and a bachelor's degree in English education. She is a wife, mother, grandmother, and great-grandmother. Spending time with family is one of her favorite pastimes. She lives in Chicago with her husband of more than five decades.

RESOURCES ONLINE

Visit the author's page to access the resources mentioned in
this book.

<u>Pressing Toward the Marks Author's Resources</u>

<u>https://centerstreetpublishing.com/pressing-toward-the-marks</u>

REFERENCES

Alberta Civil Liberties Research Center (ACLRC). (2021). *Types of racism*, Retrieved from http://www.aclrc. com/glossary)

Bell, S. (2011). *Pastoral ministry as interpretive theology*, presented at the Annual Association of Doctor of Ministry Education Conference. New Orleans, LA.

Benard, B. (2004). *Resiliency: What we have learned.* San Francisco, CA: WestEd.

Bennis, W., & Nanus, B. (1985). *Leaders: The strategies for taking charge.* New York: Harper and Row.

Brooks, J. G., & Brooks, M. G. (1993). *The case for constructivist classrooms.* Alexandria, VA: ASCD.

Burkhart, J. E. (1982). *Worship.* Philadelphia: The Westminster Press.

Burley-Allen, M. (1993). *Listening the forgotten skill.* Hoboken, NJ: John Wiley & Sons.

Clinebell, H. (2011). *Basic types of pastoral care and counseling: resources for the ministry of healing and growth* (3rd ed.). Updated by Bridget Clare McKeever. Nashville: Abingdon Press.

Cormode, S. (2013). *Overview of the theological reflection process.* Retrieved from https:// www.fuller.edu/wp-content/uploads/ 2018/08/Theological-Reflection-Overview-2013.doc

Cron, I. M., & Stabile, S. (2016). The road back to you: An Enneagram journey to self-discovery. Downers Grove, IL: InterVarsity Press.

Deal, T. E. (1990). Reframing Reform. *Educational Leadership, 47*(8), pp. 6-12.

Delecta J. R., & Raman, G. P. (2015). *Cross-cultural communication barriers in the workplace. International Journal of Management 6*(1), January (2015), pp. 348-351.

Delpit, L. (1988). The silenced dialogue: Power and pedagogy in educating other people's children, *Harvard Educational Review 58* (1988), pp. 280-298.

Diemer, M. A., Kauffman, A., Koenig, N., Trahan, E., & Chueh-An, H. (2006). *Challenging racism, sexism, and social injustice: support for urban adolescents' critical consciousness development,* Retrieved from https://pubmed. ncbi.nlm.nih.gov/16881749/

Dybahl, J. (2011). *Theological reflection.* Retrieved from: https://www.andrews. edu/sem/ dmin/about/theological-reflection/index.html

Easley, S. (2019). *The relationship between leadership style and personality type among college students.* Honors Theses. 58. Dominican University Available at: https://doi.org/ 10.33015/ dominican.edu/ 2019.HONORS.ST.16

FaithTrust Institute. *Healthy boundaries.* Retrieved from: lwww.faithtrustinstitute.org

Freire, P. (1970, 2000). *Pedagogy of the oppressed.* New York, NY: Continuum.

Fullan, M. G. (1999). *Change forces: The sequel.* Philadelphia, PA: Falmer Press.

Graham, E. (2013), Is practical theology a form of 'action research? *International Journal of Practical Theology 17*(1), pp. 148–178.

Greenleaf, R. K. (2007),.*What is servant leadership?* Retrieved from https://www.greenleaf.org/what-is-servant-leadership/

Henderson, N., & Milstein, M. M.,(2003). *Resiliency in schools: Making it happen for students and educators* (Updated ed.). Thousand Oaks, CA: Corwin Press.

Hooker, D. A. (2016). *The little book of transformative community conferencing: A hopeful, practical approach to dialogue (justice and peacebuilding)*. New York: Good Books.

Huerta, D. (2020). *Privilege walk activity*. Retrieved from http://doloreshuerta.org/wp-content/ uploads/ 2020/04/privilege-walk.pdf

Jones, D. (2009). *Theological reflection in Doctor of Ministry Education: Ten helpful lenses,* presented at the Annual Association of Doctor of Ministry Education Conference. Dallas TX.

Jones, V. L. (2009). *African American parental beliefs about resiliency: A Delphi study.* UNLV Theses/ Dissertations/Professional Papers/ Capstones. Paper 960. Retrieved from http://digitalscholarship. unlv.edu/ thesesdissertations/960

King, K. P. (2008),.Workplace performance-plus: Empowerment and voice through scholarship development and democratic processes in health care training. *Performance Improvement Quarterly, 21*(4), pp. 55-74.

Kuhn, T. S. (1970). *The structure of scientific revolutions* (2nd enlarged ed.). Chicago: University of Chicago Press.

LeBaron, M. (2003). Communication tools for understanding cultural differences. *Beyond intractability,* eds. Guy Burgess and Heidi Burgess. Conflict Research Consortium, University of Colorado, Boulder. Retrieved from http://www.beyondintractability. org/ essay/ communication_ tools/

Lewin, K. (1951). *Lewin's force field analysis*, Retrieved from https://www.mindtools.com/ pages/article/ newTED_06.htm

Lewis, S., Williams, M. W., & Baker, D. G. (2020). *Another way: Living and leading change on purpose* [Kindle iOS version]. Retrieved from Amazon.com.

Malphurs, A. (2013). *Advanced strategic planning: A 21st-century model for church and ministry leaders*, Grand Rapids, MI: Baker Books.

McIntyre, A. (2000). Constructing meaning about violence, school, and community: Participatory action research with urban youth. *The Urban Review, 32*(2), 123-154.

McKim, D. K. (2014). *The Westminster dictionary of theological terms (2nd ed.): Revised and expanded* . Westminster John Knox Press. Kindle Edition.

Meier, D. (1995). *The power of their ideas: Lessons for America from a small school in Harlem,* Boston, MA: Beacon Press.

Merriam-Webster Dictionary. (n.d.). *Worship*, Retrieved from https://www.merriam-webster.com/ dictionary/worship

Mezirow, J. (1991). *Transformative dimensions of adult learning.* San Francisco: Jossey-Bass.

Milco, Michael R. (1997). *Ethical dilemmas in church leadership: Case studies in biblical decision-making.* Grand Rapids, MI: Kregel Publications.

Mitchel, D. E. & Tucker, S. (1992, February). Leadership as a way of thinking. *Educational Leadership, 49*(5), pp. 30-35.

Newport, F. (2018, September 7). *Church leader and declining religious service attendance.* Polling Matters. https://news. gallup.com/opinion /polling-matters/242015/church-leaders-declining-religious-service-attendance.aspx

Owen, R. G. (1991). *Organizational behavior in education* (6ᵗʰ ed.). Needham Heights, MA: Viacom Company.

Patterson, K., Grenny, J., McMillan, R., & Switzler, A. (2012), *Crucial conversations: Tools for talking when stakes are high* (2ⁿᵈ edition). New York: McGraw Hill.

Reed, J. R., & Reed, L. C. (2020). *Cyber outreach: How to develop and evaluate your digital ministries*. Chicago, IL: Center Street Publishing, LLC.

Reed, L. C. (1995). *The leadership-culture dimensional screening scale: Development of a screening tool to identify transformational versus transactional executive style in settlement versus frontier school cultural settings,* Doctoral dissertation. Loyola University-Chicago.

Reed, L. C. (2020), *Praying from the bottom up*. Chicago, IL: Independently Published.

Rohr, R., & Ebert, A. (2019). *The Enneagram: A Christian Perspective*. New York: Crossroad Publishing Company.

Saphier, J., Brigda-Peyton, T., & Pierson, G. (1989), *How to make decisions that stay made,* Alexandria, VA: Association for Supervision and Curriculum Development.

Senn, F. C. (2006). *The people's work*. Minneapolis, MN: Fortress Press.

Sergiovanni, T. J. (1992). Why we should seek substitutes for leadership, *Educational Leadership, 49*(5), pp. 41-45.

Squarespace.com. (n.d.). *Types of sermons*. Retrieved from https://static1.squarespace.com.

Stringer, E. T. (1996). *Action research: A handbook for practitioners*. Thousand Oaks, CA: SAGE.

Taylor, E. W. (2008). *Transformative learning theory. New Directions for Adult and Continuing Education, 2008*(119). Available

from Wiley Subscription Services, Inc. at
http://dx.doi.org/ 10.1002/ ace.301.

Thomas, F. (2001). *Preaching as celebration: Digital lecture series and workbook*, Retrieved from https://drfrankathomas.com/

Thomas, F. (2020). *Preaching is back in style*, Retrieved from https://www.nes.edu/media/ 3753/preacing-is-back-in-style_final-presentation_200616.pdf

Thomas, S. (2021). *The raceless gospel*, Retrieved from https://racelessgospel. com/tag/the-most-segregated-hour/

Tyler, R. (1994). *Curriculum development*, Retrieved from https://education.stateuniversity. com/pages/2517/Tyler-Ralph-W-1902-1994.html

United Church of Christ. (2018). *Manual on Ministry. Ministerial Code of Ethics.* At https://www.ucc.org/ ministers_ordained-ministers-code

United Church of Christ. (1986). *Book of Worship*, New York: Office for Church Life and Leadership.

Young, C. J. (2013). Transformational learning in ministry. *Christian Education Journal, 10*(2), pp. 322-338.

Endnotes

Preface

[1] Oxford Languages Dictionary. (n.d.), "Organization," retrieved from https://languages.oup.com/google-dictionary-en/

Chapter 2

[2] R. G. Owens, (1991), *Organizational behavior in education* (6th ed.). Needham Heights, MA: Viacom Company.
[3] Owens, (1991), *Organizational behavior in education.*
[4] Kurt Lewin, *Kurt Lewin's Force Field Analysis,* (1951), Retrieved from https://www.mindtools.com/pages/article/newTED_06.htm
[5] M. G. Fullan, (1999), *Change forces: The sequel.* Philadelphia, PA: Falmer Press.

Chapter 3

[6] Scott Cormode, (2013), *Overview of the theological reflection process.* Retrieved from https://www.fuller.edu/wp-content/uploads/2018/08/Theological-Reflection-Overview-2013.doc
[7] Jon Dybahl, (2011), *Theological reflection,* Retrieved from: https://www.andrews.edu/sem/dmin/about/theological-reflection/index.html
[8] Skip Bell, (2011), *Pastoral ministry as interpretive theology,* presented at the Annual Association of Doctor of Ministry Education Conference. New Orleans, LA, Apr. 14-16, 2011.
[9] David Lee Jones, (2009), *Theological reflection in Doctor of Ministry Education: Ten helpful lenses,* presented at the Annual Association of Doctor of Ministry Education Conference. Dallas TX, Apr. 16-18, 2009.
[10] Jon Dybahl, (2011), *Theological reflection,* Retrieved from: https://www.andrews.edu/sem/dmin/about/theological-reflection/index.html
[11] Jon Dybahl. (2011), *Theological reflection.*
[12] Scott Cormode, (2013)
[13] Scott Cormode, (2013).

Chapter 4

[14] Merriam-Webster Dictionary, *Worship*, Retrieved from
https://www.merriam-webster.com/dictionary/worship
[15] United Church of Christ, (1986), *Book of Worship*, New York: Office for
Church Life and Leadership, 1.
[16] Donald K. McKim. *The Westminster Dictionary of Theological Terms, Second
Edition: Revised and Expanded* . Westminster John Knox Press. Kindle Edition.
[17] United Church of Christ, Book of Worship, 78.
[18] Frank C. Senn, (2006), *The people's work*. Minneapolis, MN: Fortress Press.
[19] Frank C. Senn, (2006).
[20] John E. Burkhart, (1982), *Worship*. Philadelphia: The Westminster Press,
93.
[21] Lorrie C. Reed, (2020), *Praying from the bottom up*. Chicago, IL:
Independently Published.
[22] "Types of Sermons." Retrieved from https://static1.squarespace.com
/static/5b1092e0620b855bae5f6b32/t/5ce454ba52a22b0001355060/1558
467771238/Types+Of+Sermons+Expositors+Collective.pdf
[23] Frank Thomas, *Preaching is back in style*, Retrieved from
https://www.nes.edu/media/3753/preacing-is-back-in-style_final-
presentation_200616.pdf
[24] Frank Thomas, (2001), *Preaching as celebration: Digital lecture series and
workbook*, Retrieved from https://drfrankathomas.com/
[25] Starlette Thomas cited Dr. King in *The raceless gospel*, Retrieved
fromnhttps://racelessgospel.com/tag/the-most-segregated-hour/

Chapter 5

[26] Howard Clinebell, (2011), *Basic types of pastoral care and counseling: resources for
the ministry of healing and growth* (3rd ed.). Updated by Bridget Clare McKeever.
Nashville: Abingdon Press; Updated, Revised edition., p. 8.
[27] Howard Clinebell, (2011), p. 46-53.
[28] Bonnie Benard, (2004), *Resiliency: What we have learned*. San Francisco, CA:
WestEd.
[29] N. Henderson, & M. M. Milstein, (2003), *Resiliency in schools: Making it
happen for students and educators* (Updated ed.). Thousand Oaks, CA: Corwin
Press. p. 7.
[30] V. L. Jones, (2009), *African American parental beliefs about resiliency: A Delphi
study*. UNLV Theses/Dissertations/Professional Papers/Capstones. Paper
960. Retrieved from http://digitalscholarship. unlv.edu/
thesesdissertations/960

[31] Delores Huerta.org, (2020), *Privilege walk activity*, Retrieved from http://doloreshuerta.org/wp-content/uploads/2020/04/privilege-walk.pdf

Chapter 6

[32] Ralph Tyler, (1994), *Curriculum development*, Retrieved from https://education.stateuniversity. com/pages/2517/Tyler-Ralph-W-1902-1994.html

[33] J. G. Brooks, & M. G. Brooks, (1993), *The case for constructivist classrooms.* Alexandria, VA: ASCD.

[34] Matthew A. Diemer, Aimee Kauffman, Nathan Koenig, Emily Trahan, Chueh-An Hsieh, (2006), *Challenging racism, sexism, and social injustice: support for urban adolescents' critical consciousness development*, Retrieved from https://pubmed.ncbi.nlm.nih.gov/16881749/

[35] D. A. Hooker, (2016), *The little book of transformative community conferencing: A hopeful, practical approach to dialogue (justice and peacebuilding).* New York: Good Books, p. 210.

[36] Paolo Freire, (1970, 2000), *Pedagogy of the oppressed.* New York, NY: Continuum.

[37] John Mezirow, (1991), *Transformative dimensions of adult learning.* San Francisco: Jossey-Bass.

[38] E. W. Taylor, (2008), *Transformative learning theory. New Directions for Adult and Continuing Education, 2008*(119). Available from Wiley Subscription Services, Inc. at http://dx.doi.org/10.1002/ace.301.

[39] K. P. King, (2008), Workplace performance-plus: Empowerment and voice through scholarship development and democratic processes in health care training. *Performance Improvement Quarterly, 21*(4), pp. 55-74.

[40] C. J. Young, (2013), Transformational learning in ministry. *Christian Education Journal,10*(2), pp. 322-338.

[41] Thomas S. Kuhn, (1970), *The structure of scientific revolutions* (2nd enlarged ed.). Chicago: University of Chicago Press.

[42] D. Meier, (1995), *The power of their ideas: Lessons for America from a small school in Harlem,* Boston, MA: Beacon Press.

[43] S. Lewis, M. W. Williams, & D. G. Baker, (2020), *Another way: Living and leading change on purpose* [Kindle iOS version]. Retrieved from Amazon.com.

[44] Lewis, Williams, & Baker, (2020).

[45] Lewis et al., (2020).

[46] ACLRC, *Types of Racism*, Retrieved from http://www.aclrc. com/glossary)

Chapter 7

[47]Michelle LeBaron, (2003), Communication tools for understanding cultural differences. *Beyond Intractability,* eds. Guy Burgess and Heidi Burgess. Conflict Research Consortium, University of Colorado, Boulder. Retrieved from http://www.beyondintractability. org/ essay/ communication_ tools/

[48]Lisa Delpit, (1988), The silenced dialogue: Power and pedagogy in educating other people's children, *Harvard Educational Review 58* (1988), pp. 280-298.

[49]R. Delecta Jenifer, & G. P. Raman, (2015), *Cross-cultural communication barriers in the workplace. International Journal of Management 6*(1), January (2015), pp. 348-351.

[50]Madelyn Burley-Allen, (1993), *Listening the forgotten skill,* John Wiley & Sons.

Chapter 8

[51]W. Bennis, & B. Nanus, (1985), *Leaders: The strategies for taking charge.* New York: Harper and Row.

[52] D. E. Mitchell, & S. Tucker, (1992, February), Leadership as a way of thinking. *Educational Leadership, 49*(5), pp. 30-35.

[53] Mitchell & Tucker, S. (1992, February), pp. 30-35.

[54]Lorrie C. Reed, (1995). *The leadership-culture dimensional screening scale: Development of a screening tool to identify transformational versus transactional executive style in settlement versus frontier school cultural settings,* Doctoral dissertation, Loyola University-Chicago.

[55] Terrence E. Deal, Reframing Reform, (1990), *Educational Leadership, 47*(8), pp. 6-12.

[56] Thomas J. Sergiovanni, (1992), Why we should seek substitutes for leadership, *Educational Leadership, 49*(5), pp. 41-45.

[57]F. Newport, (2018, September 7), *Church leader and declining religious service attendance.* Polling Matters. https://news. gallup.com/opinion /polling-matters/242015/church-leaders-declining-religious-service-attendance.aspx

[58] Robert K. Greenleaf, (2007), *What is servant leadership?* Retrieved from https://www.greenleaf.org/what-is-servant-leadership/

[59]Indeed.com. "10 Common Leadership Styles. Available at: https://www.indeed.com/career-advice/career-development/10-common-leadership-styles

[60]Samantha Easley, (2019), *The Relationship Between Leadership Style and Personality Type Among College Students*, Honors Theses. 58. https://doi.org/10.33015/dominican.edu/2019.HONORS.ST.16

[61]The Meyer's Briggs Company. (n.d.). *A positive framework for life-long people development.* Available at https://www.themyersbriggs. com/en-US/Products-and-Services/Myers-Briggs

[62]Richard Rohr, R., & Andreas Ebert, (2019), *The Enneagram: A Christian perspective*, p. 40.

[63]Ian M. Cron, & Suzanne Stabile, S. (2016). *The road back to you: An Enneagram journey to self-discovery, pp. 25-26.*

[64]Ian M. Cron, & Suzanne Stabile, S. (2016). *The road back to you: An Enneagram journey to self-discovery, p. 27.*

[65]Owens, (1991), *Organizational behavior in education.*

Chapter 9

[66]Kerry Patterson, Joseph Grenny, Ron McMillan, & Al Switzler, (2012), *Crucial conversations: Tools for talking when stakes are high* (2nd edition). New York: McGraw Hill, p. 180.

[67]Kerry Patterson, Joseph Grenny, Ron McMillan, & Al Switzler, p. 181.

[68]Kerry Patterson et al., p. 182.

[69]John Saphier, Tom Brigda-Peyton, & Geoff Pierson, (1989), *How to make decisions that stay made,* Alexandria, VA: Association for Supervision and Curriculum Development.

[70]E. Graham, (2013), Is practical theology a form of 'action research? *International Journal of Practical Theology 17*(1), pp. 148–178.

[71]E. Graham, (2013), pp. 148–178.

[72]A. McIntyre, (2000), Constructing meaning about violence, school, and community: Participatory action research with urban youth. *The Urban Review, 32*(2), 123-154.

[73]E. T. Stringer, (1996), *Action research: A handbook for practitioners.* Thousand Oaks, CA: SAGE.

[74]A. McIntyre, (2000).

[75]E. Graham, (2013).

[76]United Church of Christ, *Ministerial Code of Ethics.* Retrieved from https://www.ucc.org/ministers_ordained-ministers-code

[77]FaithTrust Institute, *Healthy Boundaries.* Available at: lwww.faithtrustinstitute.org

[78]Michael R Milco, (1997), Ethical dilemmas in church leadership: Case studies in biblical decision-making. Grand Rapids, MI: Kregel Publications.

[79] Faith Dunne, Paula Evans, & Gene Thompson-Grove. (n.d.). *Consultancy Protocol.* Coalition of Essential Schools and the Annenberg Institute for

School Reform. Retrieved from https://www.greatschoolspartnership.
org/wp-content/uploads/2016/11/Consultancy-Protocol.pdf

Chapter 10

[80]James R. Reed, & Lorrie C. Reed, (2020). *Cyber outreach: How to develop and evaluate your digital ministries.* Chicago, IL: Center Street Publishing, LLC.
[81]Aubrey Malphurs, (2013), *Advanced strategic planning: A 21st-century model for church and ministry leaders*, Grand Rapids, MI: Baker Books, 150.

Chapter 11

[82]United Church of Christ, *Manual on Ministry*, 2018.
[83]United Church of Christ, *Manual on Ministry*, 2018.

CPSIA information can be obtained
at www.ICGtesting.com
Printed in the USA
BVHW091351221221
624599BV00014B/1233